FIBERGLASS BOAT SURVEY

ARTHUR EDMUNDS

BRISTOL FASHION PUBLICATIONS, INC.
Rockledge, Florida

Published by Bristol Fashion Publications

Copyright © 1998 by Arthur Edmunds. All rights reserved.

No part of this book may be reproduced or used in any form or by any means-graphic, electronic, mechanical, including photocopying, recording, taping or information storage and retrieval systems-without written permission of the publisher.

BRISTOL FASHION PUBLICATIONS AND THE AUTHOR HAVE MADE EVERY EFFORT TO INSURE THE ACCURACY OF THE INFORMATION PROVIDED IN THIS BOOK BUT ASSUMES NO LIABILITY WHATSOEVER FOR SAID INFORMATION OR THE CONSEQUENCES OF USING THE INFORMATION PROVIDED IN THIS BOOK.

ISBN: 1-892216-07-8
LCCN: 98-074177

Contribution acknowledgments

Cover Photo: 47-foot, 42-knot sportfisherman designed and photographed by Arthur Edmunds.
Inside Graphics/Photos: by Arthur Edmunds, unless otherwise indicated.
Cover Design: John P. Kaufman.

TABLE OF CONTENTS

Introduction   Page 5

Chapter One
The Boat For Me   Page 7

Chapter Two
The Owner & The Surveyor   Page 17

Chapter Three
Fiberglass   Page 25

Chapter Four
Construction Details   Page 31

Chapter Five
Dissimilar Metals   Page 49

Chapter Six
Conducting The Survey   Page 55

Chapter Seven
Unusual Survey Problems   Page 83

Chapter Eight
The Business of Surveying   Page 89

Chapter Nine
Emergencies   Page 95

Chapter Ten
What's in a Name   Page 107

Chapter Eleven
Maintenance Procedures   Page 113

Chapter Twelve
Answers To Your Questions   Page 117

Chapter Thirteen
Final Thoughts   Page 133

Appendix One
Suppliers & Manufacturers   Page 137

Glossary   Page 143

Other Books   Page 159

About The Author   Page 165

INTRODUCTION

I have written this book to help the countless thousands of boaters, who each year, make an offer on a used boat. Many of these boaters have their hopes, of the first or next great boat in their lives, dashed when the surveyor's report is received with thousands of dollars of repairs stated in the report. They have only two choices at this time. Commit to completing the required repairs or start the entire purchase process again.

If this has happened to you or anyone you know, you are aware of the frustration this can cause. Many times the boater has taken weeks or months to find the right boat and proceed through the purchase process only to return to the beginning.

This book will eliminate that frustration. I begin by explaining the types of boat styles available and their primary functions or use. The reader is then taken through the same steps the professional will use, which must be completed to insure the boat is of the quality they desire, **before** an offer is made. This is the step which will save all the frustration. The final area of discussion concerns the interactions with the professional surveyor who will be required for financing or insurance.

I can assure you of this. If you read this book and follow the advice and steps to perform your own survey, you will not have any last minute surprises in the professional's report. You will know all the boat's faults before you have made the offer. Saving yourself all the aggravation and wasted time can only make you a relaxed boater.

Arthur Edmunds

Chapter One

THE BOAT FOR ME

Selection of a boat depends on where and how the owner is going to operate the boat. The following possibilities must be carefully considered:

  a. Is a dock available or will the boat have to be kept on a trailer?
  b. Will you be in the protected waters of a bay, river or lake? Will you sometimes be in the open ocean? How far offshore will you be?
  c. Is high speed required for water skiing or for fifty-mile offshore trips to the fishing grounds?
  d. Is there a large group of family and friends that will be sleeping on the boat?
  e. Will the boat be used for living aboard or for vacation cruising?
  f. What are the budget limitations?

There are many types and shapes of boats available. In an attempt to make the boat selection process easier, we can separate boats into three groups, depending on how they will be used.

The OPEN boat is aptly named, as it does not usually have a deck. (See Figure 1-1) It can be a sailboat or powerboat, usually under 25 feet in length. It is taken out for a few hours of fishing or for the enjoyment of being on the water. If the boat is kept on a trailer, the highway laws limit the beam to eight feet. A folding Bimini top is often used in an OPEN boat to help protect the passengers from the sun. Another cover may be used at the dock or at a mooring buoy. This prevents the boat from sinking due to rainwater and an inoperative bilge pump.

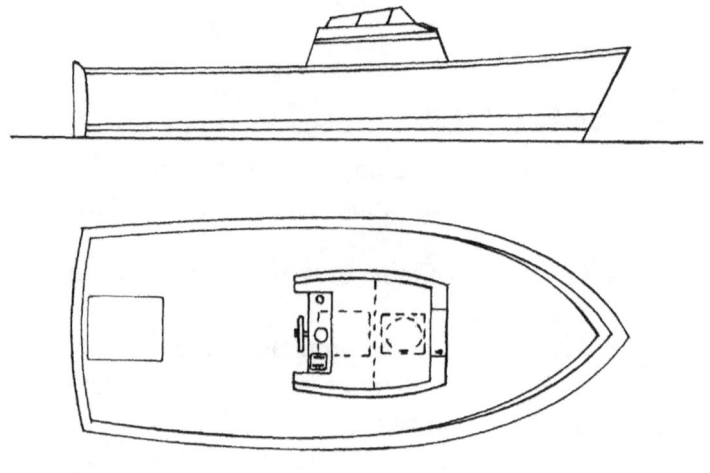

Figure 1-1

The open boat is normally less than 25 feet and the most popular type of hull.

The SEMI-ENCLOSED boat is loosely defined as one that is partially decked over in the forward half of the hull. (See Figure 1-2) It is normally between 23 and 30 feet in length and has two berths in the bow, with a toilet between. Sometimes a sink, water tank, alcohol fueled stove and lockers are installed. This is a general purpose boat that is very popular, as it has minimum accommodations for two. Operation should be limited to waves less than three feet and to winds less than fifteen knots. In open waters, a wind strength of fifteen knots starts to blow the tops off of waves and "whitecaps" are formed This boat is suitable for outboard, I/O, and inboard single or twin engines.

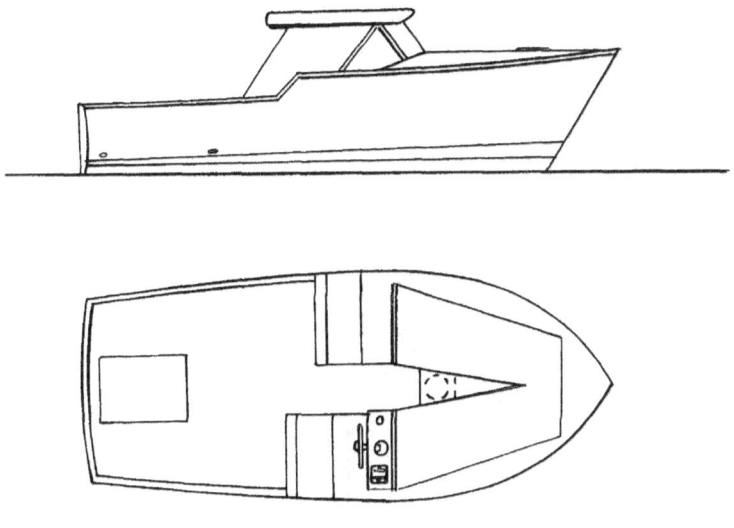

Figure 1-2

The semi-enclosed boat is usually between 23 and 30 feet, providing minimum accommodations for two.

The CRUISING boat is generally over 28 feet in length, as that is the minimum size for living aboard and reasonably comfortable cruising. There is a large galley, many berths, an enclosed head and a sitting area that converts to more sleeping berths. (See Figure 1-3) Many lockers and drawers are always appreciated. There is never enough storage space. The number of berths, heads and amount of storage depends entirely on the length of the hull and what the owner is willing to invest. Larger boats sometimes have a washer and dryer, chart desk, oilskin and boot locker, linen locker and drawers designated for each person. The addition of equipment and the conveniences of modern living are endless on a large powerboat. The cruising powerboat or sailboat is only an extension of a smaller hull. Individual preference will determine what an owner will buy.

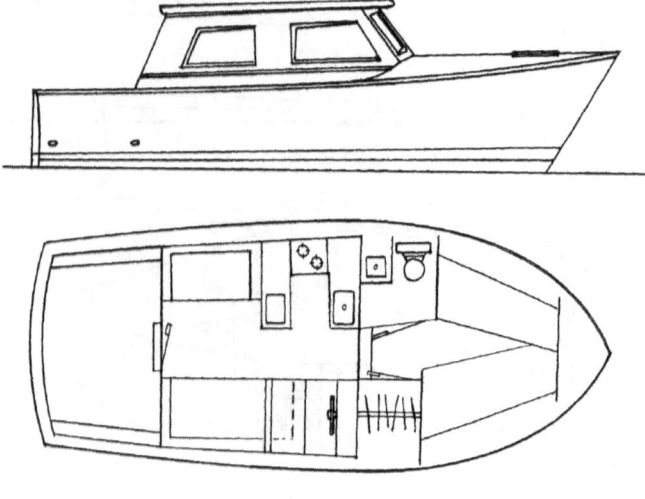

Figure 1-3

The cruising boat is usually over 28 feet. In this example, there are three berths and an enclosed helm. Larger versions can provide all the comforts of any land home.

LIVING ON BOARD

Living *large* in a small space is a good definition of living aboard a boat. It is like a small house with half the floor space. If you have many clothes, books or hobbies, living on a boat may be difficult, if the boat is less than 45 feet in length. It is a complete change of lifestyle.

Visits to others living on board will bring a clear insight to the joys and problems. Living aboard will surely cure a bad case of kindred: the fear of visiting relatives. There are many manufactured boats, both power and sail, suitable for cruising, but a large amount of safety equipment should be added in order to prepare for any emergencies. It is critical to water from entering the boat. All joints and windows must be checked with a direct stream of water from a hose to reveal any problems. If windows are large, plastic or plywood covers may be installed for long ocean passages. A small boat or life raft should be on board, plus radio communications, flares and an emergency position radio beacon (EPIRB).

Ocean crossings have been successfully completed by small powerboats with an economical diesel engine and additional fuel tanks. Most people would choose a sailboat to be independent from fuel supplies. The fuel supply is normally limited and the engine becomes a secondary, emergency means of propulsion. The size of boat selected is a matter of individual preference, but it should be understood that sailing is always more comfortable in a longer hull whose weight (displacement) is kept light by having minimum interior accommodations. On the other hand, many people who have successfully completed world cruising agree that they had few problems with repairs, docking or bureaucratic paperwork because their boat was less than forty feet in length. Some boats were ten years old, but they made sure the hull, deck, engine and rigging were in excellent condition.

Before cruising, it is wise to take a new boat on a few short trips in rough weather in order to gain confidence in the boat and yourself. In addition to emergency equipment, there should be spare parts for the engine, pumps, head, and through hull valves, as they may not be available in every port. It is wise to select an engine and installed systems that can be serviced in any country that you might visit.

CARRYING A BOAT LOAD

One of the infrequent dangers with a small boat is overloading the hull with excess cargo, fish or people. This is particularly dangerous when the cargo shifts to one side or when people crowd to one side. Freeboard is the measurement we use to indicate overcrowding. It is usually measured from the waterline to the top of the hull (sheer). If the boat has scuppers in the aft cockpit, freeboard is measured to the scuppers, even though they are only a few inches above the waterline. In every case, it is important not to reduce the freeboard by more than half when the boat is loaded.

BOAT SPEED

With reference to powerboats, they can be categorized by the speed for which their hulls are designed: displacement speed, medium speed or planing hull. The planing hull is moving at such a high speed that there is dynamic lift and the forward half of the hull is completely out of the water. Often, only the propeller is in the water. A high horsepower engine is installed that uses a great amount of fuel. High speed is always expensive, whether in a boat, car or aircraft.

The slow, displacement speed hull develops a bow and stern wave and the hull settles into the trough between these two crests. Without sufficient power to climb over its own bow wave, the hull is moving at its maximum speed. These hulls very often have a round bilge, as this shape has proven to be the most efficient for slow, displacement speeds. We sometimes see a displacement speed commercial fishing trawler or a cruising trawler yacht built with a hard corner (chine) at the intersection of the hull bottom and the hull side, instead of a round bilge. This is done by many commercial builders in wood, steel or aluminum, as a fast means of building in their particular yard.

Displacement speed hulls with a round bilge usually roll excessively in a seaway and with a beam wind, but there are passive and active stabilizers on the market to reduce this roll. The medium speed hull has enough power to climb over its own bow wave but not enough to lift the forward half of the hull.

The question becomes: What determines whether a boat is displacement, medium or planing speed before its performance is seen on the water? It is hard to make an exact classification, but the distinction can be approximated using a ratio of total boat weight divided by the total advertised horsepower of the engine(s). If the weight (displacement) divided by HP is greater than 80, the boat operates in a displacement speed mode. The word displacement is used interchangeably between weight and speed in this context only. If this ratio is between 50 and 80, the boat is usually of medium speed. When this ratio is less than 50, the boat is usually planing, with the exception of unusual or uneven loading conditions.

I have accumulated data from many boat tests and the results are tabulated in Figure 1-4. Maximum boat speed varies with the weight of the boat, efficiency of the engine and cleanliness of the hull bottom. If you conduct your own speed test, make sure you eliminate the following causes of poor boat speed:

    a. The fuel may be contaminated with dirt or water.
    b. The spark plugs are fouled (gasoline).
    c. The injectors need service (diesel).

d. The engine may not have sufficient air for proper combustion of the fuel.

 e. The propeller may be the wrong size.

 f. Barnacles may be on the hull bottom and on the propeller.

 g. The electronic "radar" gun may not be calibrated properly.

 h. The measured mile may not be accurate.

We have discussed the types and speeds of boats in order to help the owner in the boat selection process. Too often, the owner assumes the hull is fine because it is floating and assumes the engine is strong because it runs well. Next, we will look into the owner's relationship with the surveyor and how the buyer may conduct his own preliminary inspection.

Boat Weight	TOTAL ADVERTISED ENGINE HORSEPOWER								
	50	100	200	300	400	500	600	700	800	1000
3000	22	31	44	53	62	69	75	82	87	97
4000	19	27	38	46	53	60	66	71	75	84
5000	17	24	34	41	48	53	58	63	68	75
6000	15	22	31	38	44	49	53	58	62	69
7000	13	20	28	35	40	45	49	53	57	64
10000	12	17	24	29	34	38	41	45	48	53
12000	11	16	22	27	31	35	38	40	43	49
14000	10	15	20	25	29	32	35	38	40	45
16000	9.5	14	19	24	27	30	32	35	38	42
18000	9	13	18	22	25	28	31	33	36	40
20000	8.5	12	17	21	24	27	29	31	34	38
22000	8.2	11.5	16	20	23	26	28	30	32	36

24000	8	11.2	15.5	19	22	25	27	29	31	35
26000	7.6	10.8	15	18	21	23	26	28	29	34
28000	7.3	10.4	14.5	17.5	20	22.5	25	27	28.5	32
30000	7	10	14	17	19	22	24	26	28	31
35000	6	9	13	15	18	20	22	24	26	29
40000	5	8	12	14	17	19	21	22	24	27

Figure 1-4

This table shows the approximate boat speed (knots) at a given, full load boat weight (pounds) with the stated horsepower.

Photo 5

Because a shaft, strut, or rudder does not protrude from the bottom of the hull, higher-than-normal speeds are possible, with the Arneson Surface Drives from Twin Disc Inc., Racine, Wisconsin.

Chapter Two

THE OWNER AND THE SURVEYOR

After the ideal boat is selected, your thoughts naturally turn to the question of seaworthiness and quality construction. The careful buyer will patiently look at the boat and, if satisfied, will then have a professional surveyor give an impartial opinion of the quality of the boat and systems. All of this should be accomplished before buying the boat.

The most difficult part of any survey is with installed equipment and systems. It is impossible to know when an impeller on a water pump will fail or when there may be a short in a radio transmitter. All you can do is check the equipment before taking a trip.

In order to assist the buyer in conducting a preliminary survey, the following check lists have been compiled. They represent only a small part of what the professional surveyor may inspect.

THE BOAT BUYER'S INSPECTION LIST

DECK

   a. Are all cleats and lifeline stanchion bases through bolted? Screws always loosen with movement of the hardware.
   b. Are there cracks in the paint or gel coat?
   c. Check the rub rails and deck to hull joint to insure they are properly fastened.
   d. Is there an anchor and rode locker? Is there a place to stow dock lines, fenders and life jackets (pfd)?
   e. Are the navigation lights and horn working?
   f. Look for streaks of water inside windows and hatches. This indicates where they are not watertight.
   g. Are there at least two water trap type ventilators to the living area and two ventilators to the engine room area?
   h. Is the deck's non-skid surface adequate?
   i. Is there a dinghy or life raft on board?
   j. Are there provisions for emergency steering?

HULL EXTERIOR

   a. If the boat is in the water, all you can do is look for gouges and scratches in the gel coat or paint.
   b. When the boat is hauled out, look for dents or pitting on the propeller and excessive movement of the shaft bearing.
   c. If the rudder is fiberglass, is the centerline seam separated?
   d. If a sailboat, is the bolted keel or ballast slightly separated from the hull? If so, the bolts should be tightened, if possible. If not, this could be a major repair.

e. If a steel or aluminum hull, are there signs of corrosion?

f. If a wood hull, check the seams at the edge of the transom. Is the paint smooth or are there raised areas at the planking seams and at the wood plugs over fastenings?

INTERIOR
a. Remove floor hatches to check for water accumulation and find out where the water is coming in.

b. Both the hull sides and bottom must have stiffeners spaced 30 inches or less. Engine girders should continue forward to the bow.

c. Are there vented loops in both the head intake and discharge?

d. Is the toilet and discharge system working without leaks or odor?

e. Is there a fuel shut off valve near the galley stove?

f. If a centerboard sailboat, is the hoist working?

g. Is all piping supported every three feet?

h. Is the exhaust line supported every three feet?

i. Are there fire extinguishers and life jackets?

j. Is the wiring properly supported, corrosion free, with the correct connectors?

ENGINE ROOM
a. All hoses should have two hose clamps at each end.

b. Is the shaft stuffing box leaking water?

c. Can you see into the engine and generator water heat exchanger to check the water level? Can you reach the oil dipstick?

d. Are there strainers on all the sea water intake pipes?

e. Run the engine and generator to see if water is

coming out of the exhaust line at the transom. Is there smoke in the exhaust?

f. Check for oil leaks around the oil pan, on the engine and in the oil drip pan.

g. The rudder must be supported by a bracket and not just resting on the rudder stuffing box.

h. Electrical wiring must be at deck level and not in the bilge.

i. The electrical distribution box should have circuit breakers.

j. All through hull fittings must have tapered wood plugs wired or chained to them for use in an emergency, if the fitting fails.

After inspecting the boat, the buyer sometimes resents the idea of calling in someone to determine what may be wrong with it. Neither the boat broker nor the boat salesman is pleased with the surveyor, either, as he might interfere with the sale. The buyer must realize the insurance company will probably require a survey and the surveyor is really acting in the best interest of the buyer. Isn't it worth a $200 fee to find out that you are about to make a $20,000 mistake? The boat should be hauled out of the water for an exacting survey. The boat yard charges are a necessary part of determining the condition of the hull, whether or not you buy the boat.

You must have confidence in your boat and equipment. You certainly do not want to take your family and friends on the boat unless the hull and systems are in good working order. On the basis of his inspection, the surveyor will report any deficiencies and answer questions about the condition of the hull. Even if you are very experienced and inspect your boat periodically, it's always good to hire an expert. All of us can miss a detail. We need to know what requires immediate repair and what can wait until the next haul out.

SELECTING A SURVEYOR

Every boat yard, broker or sales agent works with surveyors from time to time and they can always assist the owner with a recommendation. Since you must obtain a survey for insurance purposes, it may be best to ask the insurance agent for the name of a surveyor they acknowledge. It is important the surveyor has experience with the boat in question. Some surveyors may not inspect aluminum or ferro-cement hulls, while others may not climb a sailboat mast to check the spreaders and masthead fittings. Tell the surveyor about the boat on the first phone call. If you have a specific question about your boat, make sure the surveyor knows before proceeding.

It is important for the buyer to realize the surveyor is only human and he has no magical powers to determine when a failure may occur. Most complaints about surveyors come from owners who find a cracked pipe fitting, a frozen sea cock or an electrical short a few weeks after receiving a survey report which did not list the problem. The surveyor may have missed the defect, but it is also possible that the problem did not exist at the time of the survey. The surveyor can only see the condition of the boat at the time he inspects it. Further, a problem may be hidden behind a permanent installation such as an icebox or a decorative panel.

The surveyor can be an excellent source of information for general boating questions, in addition to the condition of that particular hull. The owner should make every attempt to be present at the survey. Naturally, he should not hang over the surveyor's shoulder, but stand at a considerate distance. The surveyor will probably maintain a conversation about what he is looking for at that particular moment.

SURVEYOR'S COMMENTS

When the surveyor reports an item has deteriorated and will require replacement, he does not mean it can be postponed until it is convenient to visit the boat yard. It is the responsibility of each owner to have items repaired as required by the survey report. Examples of such items would be the leaking exhaust elbow on the engine or the rusting of a muffler in the exhaust line. The latter is extremely important, as carbon monoxide can quickly end the pleasures of boating and life.

The surveyor is often asked to estimate the life of a piece of equipment, which is an impossible question. The surveyor can only reply that any repairs should be made immediately.

I once found a badly corroded aluminum mast on a sailboat that was set in a rusting, steel mast step. I recommended immediate repair of the mast and replacement with an aluminum mast step. The prospective buyer wanted to have the work done in his home boat yard and asked if the mast would make the trip. "Only under power", I replied. It could be argued the mast was adequate for light winds, but who would want to go to sea with that problem?

The surveyor knows he must be ethical in everything he says. It is not wise to make disparaging remarks about any particular boat or owner. If there are problems with one type of manufactured boat, it is best to discuss the problem without naming the builder. The surveyor wants to be as helpful as possible to the owner and broker, as they are a potential source of future business, but any defects can be discussed in a positive manner.

The survey report may contain pages of details about what is not functioning and what hull repairs are needed. The length of the report is often an indication of how thorough an inspection was made, but a long report does not necessarily mean a bad boat. Each report must be studied to determine what are merely cosmetic deficiencies that are easily fixed, and what are dangerous or costly mechanical defects. The summary of the report should indicate how these defects can be repaired, unless a specialized mechanic is required.

BOAT PRICES

When the survey report shows items to be repaired, the owner usually asks the surveyor what should be done and how much will it cost. The surveyor really has no idea what a boat yard will charge. He can only tell the owner his experience with similar boats. If the owner wants to know the cost of repair to use as leverage in negotiations with the seller, he should first go to the boat yard and not involve the surveyor.

The prices of new boats can be compared in the usual manner. A few visits to the dealers will make the buyer an expert on what is currently available.

Prices of used boats are a far different matter. The costs of used boats vary with many factors; age, condition, location in the USA, eagerness of the seller, reputation of the builder and the uniqueness of a custom hull.

Often, newspaper and magazine ads will give a clue as to the price range of similar boats. It is hard to make a general statement about the determination of boat prices. Two identical boats may be priced $15,000 apart if one is in Florida and one is in Minnesota.

Condition is probably the most important factor in boat pricing. If a surveyor determines an engine is expelling black smoke in the exhaust, the refrigeration is not working or there is an odor of fuel in the bilge, the boat price may be reduced by half. Economic conditions may severely change prices, as we saw in 1973 when fuel prices were dramatically increased. Inflation since that time has caused some twenty-year-old boats to sell for more than the original purchase price. Comparison shopping is necessary.

Chapter Three

FIBERGLASS

Most of this discussion of surveying boats will concentrate on glass hulls, as this material is the most common used in boat construction for the past thirty years. I started going out on fiberglass boats in 1950 and many of these hulls are still being used, if they have been properly maintained. Although, many of the early "glass" hulls have been abandoned, not because of the hull material but because the engine and interior deteriorated.

Glass hulls have proven to be very durable and require little maintenance. These are the primary reasons glass fiber is in demand all over the world. The material is corrosion resistant and provides a strong structure with light weight. The very long life of glass hulls has brought the question of how do you dispose of them when no one wants to rebuild the interior? Fortunately, the recycling industry has found a good use for old boat hulls. They are now ground into small pieces and used as filler material in the paving of roads and in products made of plastic composites.

Long fibers of glass are cut, woven and knitted into

various cloth-like materials. When these materials are saturated with a liquid resin, of which there are many types, there is a chemical reaction that forms a hard, but slightly flexible laminate. Thickness can be varied by adding as many layers as is necessary to increase strength and reduce flexibility. If the glass cloth and resin are combined in the complex shape of a mold, the laminate will faithfully reproduce that exact shape.

Normally, a manufacturer will use alternating layers of glass MAT and WOVEN ROVING, as this combination produces the thickest laminate at the lowest cost.

MAT consists of short strands of glass fiber held loosely in a sheet with a binder. It must be carefully handled to keep from pulling apart.

WOVEN ROVING is a coarse weave of long glass fibers, usually with equal number of fibers in each direction. This material is a heavy, white fabric that provides most of the strength of the finished laminate. Unidirectional fabric may be purchased for special applications.

There are many other types of glass fiber, aramid fiber, and carbon fiber materials available for boat construction, but the two mentioned above are the most common in manufacturing practice. There are also many formulations of resin used with the glass material, but the lower cost polyester resin is the most prevalent. Epoxy resin is used widely for secondary bonds inside the hull and for repairs to the hull after damage. Secondary bonds refer to attachment of bulkheads to the hull, cabin sole to the hull or overlay on the inside of the deck to hull joint.

The liquid resin hardens when the laminate is manufactured, but this resin will burn if there is a fire. The glass fiber material will not burn. A fire retardant can be added to the resin to suppress burning or a fire-retardant paint can be used on the interior of the hull. The exterior of the hull has a gel coat of higher quality resin that provides a glossy finish and prevents water from seeping into the glass laminate underneath. This gel coat resists ultraviolet deterioration from the sunlight, but it can become chalky if not waxed every six months. Sunlight works against most materials except metal.

Since the glass laminate is essentially man made, the quality and resultant strength properties can vary with the materials used, the skill of the laminator, and the technique used by the manufacturer. In actual practice, the quality control can be very strict or nonexistent. For this reason, the strength of any laminate can only be determined by having a sample tested in an engineering laboratory. This testing should be repeated every six months to insure the laminating crew has not changed their procedures. These tests show the strength of the completed laminate which is used in the calculations for determining hull thickness. This should not be confused with the advertised strength of the basic synthetic fibers, which may be many times the flexural strength of the finished laminate.

Glass fiber laminates have two properties that must be kept carefully under control. The finished laminate is quite flexible in the thickness normally used in boat hulls. Frames (stiffeners) must be added that are spaced 20 to 30 inches apart, depending on the length of the boat. There have been many cases of excessive flexing in the bow areas of both powerboats and sailboats when stiffeners were not installed. Also, the glass laminate is very apt to delaminate if water is allowed to enter the edges. On a boat hull, these edges are normally only at the sheer, where the deck is attached to the hull and where any hole is cut into the hull for through hull fittings. These bare edges must be sealed with epoxy resin, applied in two or more coats. The first coat will be quickly absorbed and epoxy resin must be added until all of the individual fibers are coated. In addition, caulking compound must be used when the fitting is installed or when the deck is put on the hull. Water must be kept away from the glass laminate.

Both custom and manufactured boats are built of glass fiber because of durability and ease of maintenance. Builders who can afford the high initial cost of molds find that labor hours are less than with other materials and the completed boat can be sold at a competitive price. Custom glass hulls that are built without a mold must be tediously sanded on the outside to achieve an acceptable surface finish. One exception to this is the custom "V" bottom hull fabricated from full length sheets of glass laminate that have the gel coat finish on one side.

ATTACHMENT OF THE INTERIOR

The bulkheads (partitions) inside the boat divide the hull into areas of privacy but they provide the more important function of stiffening the hull so that it will not bend or twist in a seaway. These bulkheads, counter tops, edges of berths and the edges of flooring all must be secured to the hull by overlaying each with twelve inch wide strips of glass MAT and WOVEN ROVING. Three pair, three of each material, should be used. Each surface must be clean and sanded to a rough finish to get a secure bond. All of these attached edges should be inspected to insure they have not separated due to the motion of the hull.

In addition, the hull must be stiffened under the flooring (cabin sole) where there are not bulkheads. This is accomplished by bringing the engine girders as far forward as possible and adding stiffeners outboard of these supports. Twenty to thirty inches should be the largest span between these stiffeners. In some hulls there is a glass fiber inner liner that is molded partially to the shape of the hull and partially to the location of interior joinerwork. In this case, the hull liner is secured with a special adhesive and is overlaid to the hull with glass laminate at its edges.

CORE MATERIALS

In an effort to save weight, some glass fiber laminates, particularly in the deck, use a core material sandwiched between two solid glass laminates. Not surprisingly, this is called 'sandwich' construction. It produces the same strength and stiffness, but with lighter weight. There are many types of core materials available, including, end grain balsa wood, urethane foam, PVC foam and various forms of honeycomb shaped material. All have proven to work well and it is cost and the preference of the builder that determines which is used.

Great care must be used in fabrication to insure the core is perfectly bonded to the glass laminate on both sides. At the edges of the deck and hull sides, the core material is stopped a few inches from the edge and the outer and inner glass laminates are brought together so the deck can be strongly attached to the hull.

Core construction is widely used in decks and sometimes in the hull sides, but there is great controversy about using cores in the bottom of the hull. There have been cases where the core in the bottom has been crushed by continued pounding while being transported on a trailer. Boat yards cannot tell when a hull bottom is of core construction. A boat yard crew may haul the boat and set it on only two keel blocks. This causes an excessive load on the core and it fails. In addition, each through hull fitting must go through a solid laminate so the bolts may be tightened without danger of crushing a core. It is very tedious and expensive to remove a core material and replace it with solid laminate at through hull fittings.

When core construction is used in the deck, great care must be used when installing the bolts for hardware. Stainless steel pipe spacers, cut exactly to the thickness of laminate and core, must be installed so the core is not crushed. These compression tubes are slightly larger than the bolt diameter on their inside diameter and are set in epoxy glue to keep the water out. Inside the laminate, an aluminum backing plate, about three-sixteenths of an inch thick, is used to spread the bolt load.

Chapter Four

CONSTRUCTION DETAILS

We will confine this discussion to glass fiber boats and categorically state that if you want to reinforce a glass hull or attach interior shelves or brackets, the job should be done with additional glass laminate. Whenever metals are used in a glass hull, they have to be bolted. Screws do not hold well in glass fiber and will loosen with time, even if the screw is bedded in epoxy glue. Some construction areas that are most difficult include the propeller shaft tube as it passes through the hull. Here a glass tube with about half inch wall thickness is held in place with epoxy glue and is reinforced inside the hull with one inch of glass laminate. When we discuss the addition of laminate overlay, we always use alternating layers of MAT and WOVEN ROVING. Approximately ten layers (five pair) will result in one inch of finished laminate. (See Figure 4-1)

The rudder post is installed in a similar manner. Also, the same type of construction is used when a 'sea chest' is desired in a large hull. This is shown in Figure 4-2 and is merely a glass pipe projecting vertically into the engine room as the only sea water source for cooling the engines, generators and supply water for the watermaker. This eliminates many through hull penetrations. This 'sea chest' standpipe is about a foot higher than the waterline or heeled waterline in a sailboat, so any debris may be removed. A pipe cap or plastic sheet with hose clamps covers the top. Short lengths of glass pipe are epoxy glued to the side of the "sea chest" to attach hoses for directing the water to the equipment. Be sure to use two hose clamps for each attachment.

As an alternative to the glass fiber sea chest, a two inch or larger through hull fitting can be installed with a seacock and a copper pipe used to form the vertical water chamber. A pipe cap is used at the top and smaller copper pipes are brazed to the sides. The pipe must be braced to the hull or bulkhead.

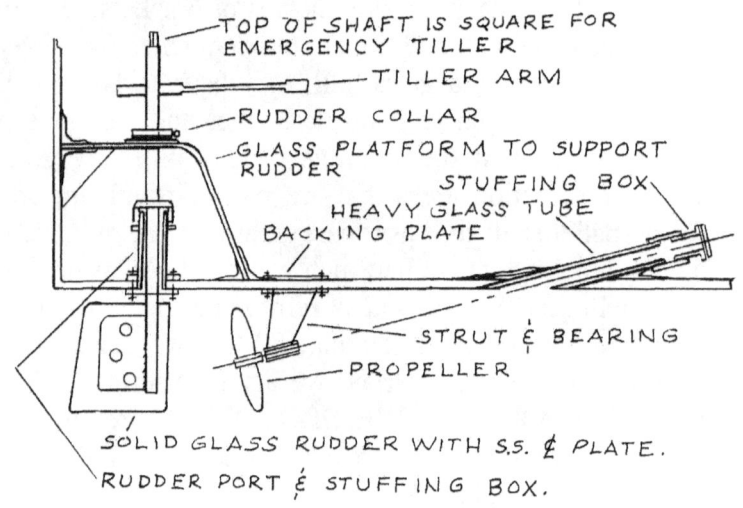

Figure 4-1

Construction detail of the shaft tube and stuffing box. Also shown is the rudder port and foundation.

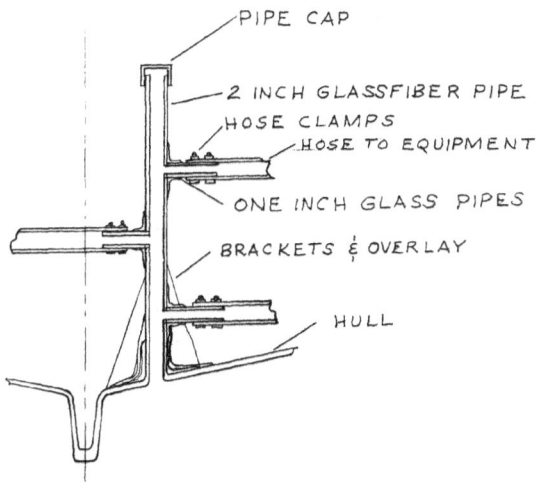

Figure 4-2

Construction detail of a glass "seachest" to facilitate the use of one hull opening for all the sea water piping. A conventional through hull fitting with a seacock and copper pipe may be used in a glass or wood hull. Other hull materials must use the same material as the hull for the construction of the seachest.

CUSTOM HULLS

When only a few hulls are planned, it is too costly to build a mold in the normal manner. Instead, the hull is laminated over a male 'plug' that is expendable and looks just like a wood hull before it is planked. The wood frames of the plug are connected with longitudinal stringers spaced about four inches apart and the entire surface is covered with a plastic sheet to prevent the glass from sticking to the wood framework. In some cases, the builder prefers to partially plank the plug with wood veneers.

The fiberglass laminate is built up on this plug to the desired thickness, using great care with each ply so the surface is fair and smooth. Any high spots are immediately sanded to eliminate compounding of the error. The application sequence of the glass plies must be carefully planned before lamination is started, since the required thickness varies in different areas of the hull and especially at the keel and keel sides.

When the lamination is completed, the outside surface is rough, showing some high spots and a general lack of fairness. Many hours are required to fill the low spots with a mixture of small glass beads (micro balloons) and resin. The entire hull is carefully sanded to achieve a perfectly smooth finish. After application of priming coats, the hull is painted with a gel coat, epoxy or polyurethane paint. (See Figures 4-3 and 4-4)

Figure 4-3

The custom glass hull will be laminated over this wood plug.

Figure 4-4

Finished 38 foot fiberglass hull for a shoal draft centerboard sailboat.

MANUFACTURING TECHNIQUES

When a large number of identical hulls are to be made, a glass cavity mold is prepared. First a wood plug is constructed exactly like a wood hull and the cavity mold is taken from this wood plug. This plug may be a finished custom glass hull, a wood boat or a hull built of some other material. It is illegal to take a mold from another manufacturer's boat! A perfect finish is applied to the plug and it is waxed and sprayed with a mold release film so the parts will not stick. The mold gel coat is then sprayed onto the plug, followed by one inch of glass laminate. The curing of any glass laminate will give off heat from the chemical reaction and the mold will have to be securely braced to prevent it from warping out of shape. Before removal from the plug, the mold is reinforced on the outside with steel or aluminum pipe welded into a solid framework. Often, a trunnion is welded to each end of the framework so that the mold can be pivoted. This allows the shop laminators to reach all areas of the mold.

After the mold is removed from the plug, many hours are required to wet sand and wax the mold interior surface. It is very important to get a high gloss where the hulls will be laminated. The releasing film is then applied and the hull color gel coat is sprayed into the mold. Laminating the hull then proceeds, as previously described. The deck mold is fabricated in a similar manner. Preparing the mold and laminating the hull requires about five working days for a forty foot hull, in comparison with ten weeks for a custom glass hull. These times will vary with each manufacturer.

Combining glass material and resin in a mold is called contact molding or hand lay-up. The laminate is cured without pressure or heat. This method is widely used. Some manufacturers prefer to place a vacuum bag (plastic sheet) over the inside of the fresh laminate and a pump is used to provide a partial vacuum. This procedure insures even distribution of the resin and it is combined with equipment to prevent resin vapors from being released to the atmosphere.

Most manufacturers prefer to have a hull mold in one piece so that there are no mold seams reproduced onto the hull, which would require refinishing of the gel coat. This is only possible if there are no inward turning hull sides (tumblehome) or other inward projections that would prevent removal from a one-piece mold.

Sometimes, a high degree of hull styling demands many inward turning shapes, recessed portlights, molded rub rails and other complex forms that distinguish a finished product. This is where two, three or more mold pieces are a must. In these cases, the mold parts are bolted together, the hull is molded and the mold parts are removed to whatever direction is necessary to clear the new hull.

Decks and superstructures are often very complex in shape and more than one piece may be molded. The pattern of seams must be carefully planned so the resulting seam compound and trim pieces do not detract from the overall styling. Flat, glass surfaces are too flexible and it is better to mold in compound curves to present high styling and stiff products.

DECK MOLDINGS

Probably the most visible problem with glass decks is very fine cracks in the gel coat, especially at corners and around hardware. High stress can cause these hairline cracks at cleats or anchor windlasses whenever there is repeated flexing of the deck laminate. These faults may be visually disturbing but are usually not serious unless the cracks enlarge to the point where there is a definite opening in the gel coat or paint. This is where the experience of a surveyor can be invaluable. Repairs are made by grinding and filling with epoxy glue and refinishing the gel coat.

These fine cracks in the gel coat often occur when the corner radius is too small, resulting in a concentration of stress. Where there are openings for a hatch or windlass, the corners should have a large radius. The same line of thinking is true for a corner in a cockpit, where the cabin side meets the deck and where a molded seat meets the seat back. (See Figure 4-5) No radius of a molded corner should be less than one inch, and three inches is preferable when it can be accomplished.

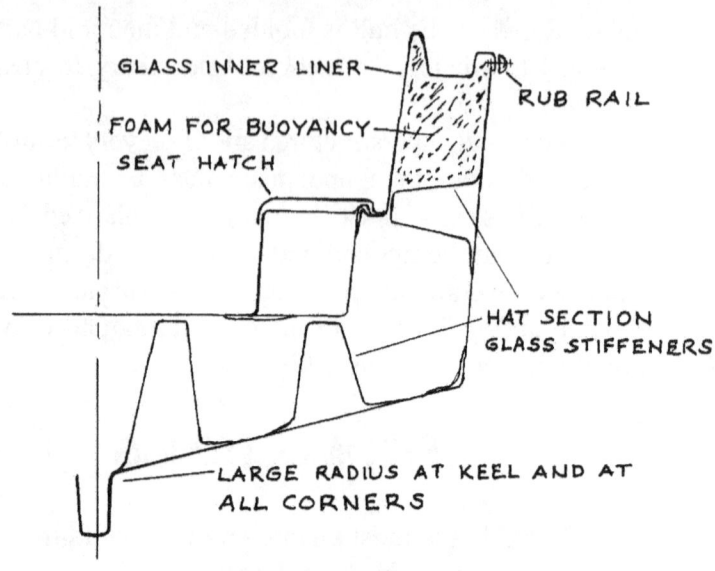

Figure 4-5

Typical glass construction with glass inner liner, hat section stiffeners and foam floatation.

This is a good place to insert a word of caution. Some boats have been made with a laminate composed entirely of MAT and resin. These hulls have little strength and have failed in service. An all MAT laminate is used in the manufacture of nonstructural parts in industries other than boating, as costs can be greatly reduced. As with any method or material, it can be misused without careful engineering.

The deck and cabin top should have sufficient support to provide minimal flexing. This support is provided primarily by bulkheads that extend full height. Additional deck beams should be installed where the span between supporting bulkheads is greater than seven feet. Often, these beams are installed longitudinally and recessed into the tops of bulkheads. The top of each bulkhead should be secured to the bottom of the deck with glass overlay. Where this is impossible, epoxy glue can be used. It is often difficult to see if the bulkheads are secured to the deck, as there may be a glass or vinyl head liner to give a pleasing finish.

In a rough sea or when the boat takes a hard roll against the dock, the hull side may be pushed inward, which in turn pushes the deck upwards, when the top of the bulkhead is not fixed. This cabin top movement frequently occurs in sailboats when sailing to windward and when tie rods are not installed between the cabin top and the keel.

As any boat pitches, rolls or yaws in a seaway, the racking stresses on the hull and superstructure are applied in different directions and especially to the cabin side and roof. The house sides (or cabin sides) are particularly vulnerable when they have large windows, little framing and a flying bridge above. Bulkheads, tie rods and extra framing are especially important in this case, but they are often neglected in favor of a large, open cabin. An alternative reinforcing procedure requires the addition of deck beams glassed to the underside of the roof with the ends glassed to vertical posts. These posts are glassed to the cabin side and extend down until they intersect the hull. This forms a strong arch structure, spaced four feet apart, throughout the length of the cabin. Shake, rattle, and roll are not for boat structures.

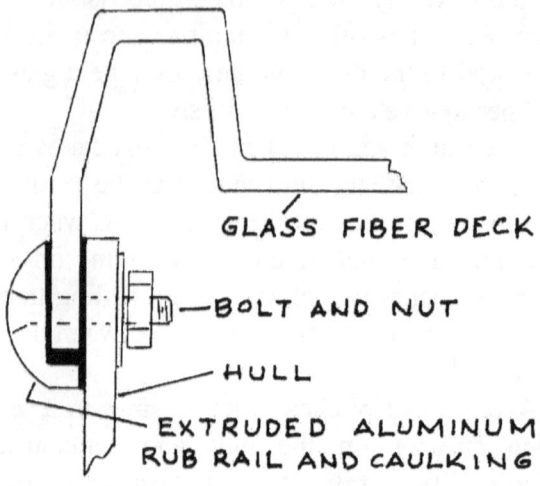

Figure 4-7

The deck to hull joint at the rub rail must be inspected carefully. This joint can be the source of constant problems if it is not properly constructed, attached and sealed.

SAILBOATS

Masts, rigging, ballast and special hardware distinguish sailboats from powerboats, but the basic structure is the same. The mast and wire rope that supports it should be free of corrosion and all fittings on the mast must be securely bolted with cotter pins to keep the bolts from loosening. The spreaders hold the upper shrouds away from the mast and prevent it from bending at the point of attachment. These spreaders are vital and must be inspected annually for corrosion or rot.

The wire rope rigging is attached to the hull by stainless steel straps called chainplates. They are bolted through the hull at the bow and stern, but pass through the deck at the sides and are bolted to knees that are heavily glassed to the hull and deck. In all cases, there must be backing plates under the nuts and washers. The hull and deck should be locally reinforced in the vicinity of the chainplates with three alternating layers (pairs) of laminate at least twelve inches in width. Bedding compound is applied under a stainless steel cover plate where each side chainplate passes through the deck.

If the sailboat has an inner jibstay in addition to the headstay, it must be secured to the hull or to the forepeak bulkhead with a strap or rod. The load should never bear on the deck alone. The tack plates for all jibs are bolted through the deck with compression tubes at all bolts. These have backing plates made from bent flat bar straps. These straps are bent to fit the chainplate bolts also, and thus transmit the tack plate load to the hull.

Sometimes it is possible to use stainless steel U-bolts to attach the rigging turnbuckles to the deck in a small sailboat. The diameter of these bolts should be twice that of the rigging to which it is attached. Under the deck, these U-bolts have to be secured to the hull or to knees that are glassed to the hull with three pairs of laminate.

If a sailboat mast is stepped on deck, it must be over a bulkhead or supporting wood structure, or on a pipe. There is a high compression load on the mast and this must be transmitted to the keel. If the deck is sandwich construction, there must be a solid laminate under the mast step.

MAST STEPS

The mast compression load on the bottom of the hull varies widely with the amount of sail area, wind strength and sailing angle to the wind. This compression load can be greater than the weight of the boat. For this reason, the load must be distributed over an area at least eighteen inches by thirty inches on a forty foot hull. The mast platform can be easily made in a glass hull by laminating inside the hull to a thickness that provides the necessary flat surface area.

Usually, it is desirable to let a free flow of water in the bilge, past the mast step to the bilge pump. This is accomplished by placing a plastic pipe on the hull before the mast platform is laminated. The mast actually sits in an aluminum collar that is welded to a flat plate. The aluminum plate is glassed to the glass mast platform. There are drain holes in the collar to prevent corrosion of the mast.

The mast step should never be made of steel, as it rusts and promotes a very tight bond with the aluminum mast. In fact, it is good practice to stay away from mild steel in any area of a glass fiber hull, with the exception of the engine and generator mounts. I witnessed a forceful example of dissimilar metals when a sailboat mast had to be removed for shipment of the boat. The rigging was freed and a crane began to lift the mast, but the crane operator wisely stopped when he realized that the entire boat was being lifted from the water. On investigation, it was found that corrosion was so advanced at the steel mast step that it had to be removed from the platform and a sledgehammer used to remove it from the bottom of the aluminum mast.

The lead ballast in a glass sailboat must be bolted on the outside of the hull in the conventional manner or it may be placed inside the hull laminate where the thickness has been increased by fifty percent. The lead inside ballast may be in one or more pieces or it may consist of lead shot secured to the hull with polyester resin. In all cases, the ballast should be covered with three pairs of glass laminate to prevent water from draining between the ballast and the hull. Any water inside the hull may freeze in the winter and expansion may damage the laminate.

The centerboard in a sailboat may be of various shapes, weights and sizes. It presents one of the most important structural problems on the boat. When the board is lowered, the water pressure on the side of the blade exerts a large force on that portion of the blade, which is inside the hull and on the watertight trunk that houses the entire assembly. In addition, the rolling of the boat in a seaway will push the board to one side and then the other, possibly loosening any weak joints. The clearance between the board and the trunk should be reduced to a minimum with stainless washers. The centerboard trunk must be very strongly laminated into the slot in the hull, as shown in Figure 4-6. The top of the trunk should extend above the waterline with an inspection plate for removal of any debris.

Some sailboats have used very heavy bronze centerboards in an effort to lower the center of gravity and improve stability. This heavy board also produces high stresses in a seaway and a solid glass centerboard is preferred for safety. A glass fiber laminate weighs about 96 pounds per cubic foot, as compared with salt water, weighing 64 pounds per cubic foot. The real purpose of the centerboard is to reduce leeway when going to windward, in a shallow draft sailboat. A wood board must be weighted so that it will sink.

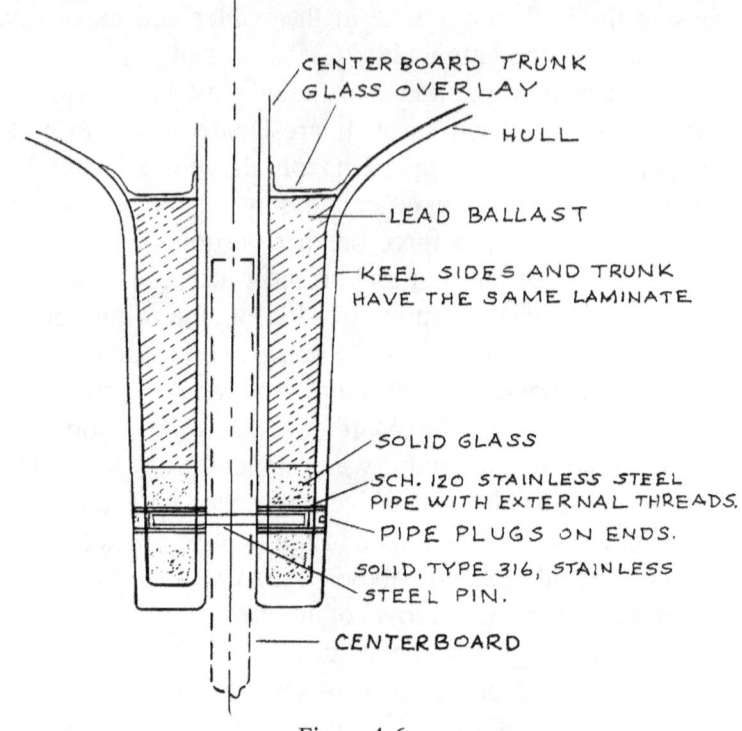

Figure 4-6

Construction detail of a centerboard installation in a shallow draft sailboat. The pin is located at the forward, lower corner of the centerboard.

The following photos show some of the equipment and the molds used in the manufacturing of a fiberglass boat.

Photo 1

Interior bow section of a fiberglass powerboat mold showing additional sheer height was added. The spots are repairs to the mold after a hull had adhered to the mold.

Photo 7

This photo shows the exterior of a fiberglass powerboat mold with steel bracing. The foreground equipment is used to spray resins and gel coat.

Photo 6

A fiberglass powerboat hull with only the bottom stiffeners installed.

Photo 2

A sailboat mold with steel bracing.

Photo 3

A fiberglass sailboat deck mold showing the complexity of shapes.

Chapter Five

DISSIMILAR METALS

Any discussion of construction details would be incomplete without some mention of what type of metals is normally used in the marine environment. The surveyor is always asking himself if the metal he is looking at is proper for the application. Electrochemical action corrodes certain metals when in the presence of other metals and water. This is commonly called galvanic corrosion or electrolysis. One metal is corroded and the other protected, depending on the type of metal and the surface area.

An example of this action would be a bronze propeller on a steel or aluminum hull. Bronze or any copper alloys should never be used with steel or aluminum as the latter will be corroded, however, the area of the metal hull is so much larger than the small bronze propeller that little corrosion occurs. Still, it is necessary to use many zinc blocks attached to the steel or aluminum hull to prevent corrosion from starting. Why zinc? It is an inexpensive metal that corrodes quicker than any other metal, and the annual replacement of zinc blocks is considered a normal part of maintenance with a metal hull.

There are some strange occurrences around docks where there are small magnitude, stray electrical currents in the water. This can also cause a form of electrochemical corrosion. Often, a bronze propeller will appear to have a bright, almost pink color and there will be pits on the surface where the zinc in the bronze alloy has been removed by this corrosion.

Marine corrosion by galvanic action is a very complicated subject that can occur in different forms. Fortunately, we don't see corrosion of a glass fiber hull except around the propeller shaft and propeller when the boat is kept at a dock. One unusual event occurred some years ago when a bottom paint containing graphite was used to try to get a slippery and fast surface. The graphite corroded the propeller shaft and the paint was discontinued. The following list is presented, in a simplified form, to show what is protected and what metals are corroded. The most protected metals are at the top and the most corroded metals are at the bottom. A brief explanation follows:

COMMON METALS USED ON BOATS

Mercury
Graphite (Carbon)
Platinum
Titanium
Stainless Steel (Type 316) Passivated

Nickel - Copper Alloys   (Inconel trademark)
Stainless Steel (Type 302 & 304) Passivated
Silver
Lead
Copper - Nickel Alloys (Monel trademark)
Bronze alloys
Brass alloys
Copper
Tin
Stainless Steel alloys; Active. No surface treatment.
Mild steel and Cast Iron
Aluminum Alloys
Zinc and Galvanized steel
Magnesium

Starting at the top of the list, we know Mercury compounds are very toxic and they have been banned from all paints and any commercial use. Mercury is so dangerous that it is even forbidden in thermometers. It is also corrosive to all other metals.

Carbon compounds are found everywhere and are mostly gasses which are easily dispersed. But in the solid state, such as graphite, they are very corrosive and act like a metal, in that they are good conductors of electricity. If graphite packing is used in the propeller shaft stuffing box, the shaft will be pitted.

High quality stainless steels have the surface treated with chemicals to reduce the chance of corrosion. These are found in the best deck hardware, propeller shafts and lifeline stanchions. Since the surface area of these parts is small compared with the area of a steel or aluminum deck or hull, the risk of corrosion is small. Stainless steel alloys are used extensively on sailboats for rigging and for hardware on the aluminum mast.

Metal alloys containing Nickel and Copper are

alloyed in various formulations and are primarily used for tubing in engine heat exchangers or air conditioning condensers. The best quality plastic valves and fittings should be used to connect this equipment, as brass fittings from some sources have been found to be of the wrong alloy.

Bronze alloys containing copper, tin and zinc have proven to be the most durable of the metals. Ancient wrecks reveal perfectly preserved statues, fittings and cannon of bronze and copper, while cast iron parts have been corroded to extinction. Do not use bronze with steel or aluminum.

Careful selection of metal hardware is important to prevent corrosion. The preference for glass fiber hulls is well justified, as the corrosion problem is eliminated. At times, a custom glass fiber hull or a steel hull will have an aluminum deck house and superstructure. This method is used to lower the center of gravity of the steel hull by using a lighter weight material above the sheer. The aluminum house is used on the custom glass hull, as many builders think it is less expensive than fabricating a custom glass structure. It is very practical on a glass hull, as the corrosion problem is nonexistent. The aluminum house is merely bolted to the glass hull with bedding compound and stainless steel bolts. Since steel and aluminum should be insulated from each other, a plastic washer plate can be used between bolted flanges.

The engine room can be the greatest source of corrosion on a glass fiber boat and most of this is probably due to just plain rusting of steel parts. When water drips from engine hatches that do not have drain grooves, all of the equipment below is subject to rusting. Look for these leaks and try to repair the source.

Chemical corrosion in the exhaust system is always a headache. Sulfur in the exhaust gas can produce sulfuric acid that corrodes the exhaust elbow, where the exhaust leaves the engine and where sea water from the heat exchanger is injected into the exhaust gasses. Careful inspection every six months will show when a replacement elbow is required.

Chapter Six

CONDUCTING THE SURVEY

Inspecting a boat is like checking an anchor chain or line; you look at each square inch and try to find the weakest link. It is impossible to find any defects by making a quick look at the deck or cabin side. The surveyor's job is to locate problems and determine if they are dangerous or merely cosmetic. This procedure takes time and the surveyor cannot be rushed to complete an inspection at a certain hour. One cynical seller was present at a survey and asked me, "Are you looking for pocket lint?" Actually, the surveyor is looking for the smallest detail and he cannot assume anything is correct. Everything is suspect until proven otherwise. "Murphy's Law" applies particularly to boats: If anything can go wrong, it will!

The surveyor should concentrate on one small area of hull, piping, or engine; make a decision; and then move on to an adjacent small area. Often, parts of the hull cannot be seen because of tanks, shower enclosures, a stove or an icebox blocking the view. These areas should be noted on the survey report, as it is just as important to know what the surveyor could NOT inspect, as to know what he did look at.

It is good practice to put your hands on and trace the various systems in the boat. For example, the fuel lines should be traced to the engine and filters, shut off valves and to the fuel fill and vent on deck. All piping should be supported every thirty inches to prevent damage by hitting other equipment. Piping at bulkheads should have rubber or watertight sleeves.

Most surveyors use a check-off list as merely a reminder to look at all the equipment and to be certain nothing is overlooked. The names of manufacturers and size of the equipment is usually noted for the owner's reference. (See Figure 6-1) These forms are convenient but do not themselves form a complete survey. Every inch of the hull and deck must be inspected.

Since the surveyor cannot be an expert in all systems, he very often notes a certain piece of equipment should be checked by a qualified serviceman. Probably the most important documentation of the survey is the written report of the surveyor's comments. (See Figure 6-2) This is what the buyer and the insurance company really want to see.

A SAMPLE CHECK LIST FOR SURVEYS
Figure 6-1
Survey for
Boat Name
Date
Location
Boat Type
Monohull or Multihull L.O.A.
L.W.L
Beam
Draft
Hull Color
Cabin Color
Year Built
State/Doc. Number
USCG H.I. No.
Home Port
Designer
Builder

SAILBOAT DATA
Ballast type
Centerboard
Type of Rig
Mast Material
Rigging Material
Type of Reefing
Number of Sails
Condition of Sails
Sail Covers
Boom Material

ENGINEROOM DATA
Engine type
No. of Engines
Year Installed
Engine Model
Manufacturer
Horsepower
Reduction Gear
Shaft Size
Shaft Material
Propeller Type

Winches

HULL EXTERIOR
Material
Condition
Frames
Flexibility
Keel Bottom
Transom
Fastenings
Through hulls
Paint, Topsides
Paint, Bottom
Blisters

DECK
Material
Condition
Rails
Windlass
Anchors
Non-skid
Cleats
Rub Rail & Joint
Cabin Material
Portlights

DECK
Dinghy
Navigation Lights
Lifelines, Stanchions
Bow & Stern Rail

INTERIOR
Life Jackets

Strut & Bearing
Shaft Stuffing Box
Rudder Support
Stuffing Box
Steering Type
Emergency Steering
Air Blower
Engine Beds
Engine Pan
Exhaust Line
Muffler
Sea Cocks
Bilge Pumps
Copper Bonding System
Fire Extinguishers
Shore Power
Generator Type
Model, KW
Battery Charger
Watermaker
Appliances
Battery Boxes
Battery Ventilation
Electrical Wiring
Circuit Breakers
Grounded Fill Pipe

ENGINEROOM
Fuel tank size, Material
Water tank size, Material

EQUIPMENT LIST
Davits on Deck
Shower Sump Pump
Air Conditioning

Buckets
Flares
Bilge water
Bulkheads
Joinerwork
Ventilation
Galley Stove
Stove Insulation
Fuel Shutoff
Refrigeration
Hot Water
Toilet Type
Vented Loops
Toilet Valves
Shower
Number of Berths
Wardrobe
Drawers
Hull Side Covering
Overhead Covering
Shore Polarity Indicator
Chart Desk
Oilskin Locker

Fans
Charts
RDF
Radiotelephone
EPIRB Emergency Beacon
Fathometer
Speedometer
Wind Direction
Compass
Loran
Radar
Bell & Horn
Barometer
Searchlight
Autopilot
Boarding Ladder
Fenders
Cabin Heater
Screens
Cockpit Awning
Holding Tank

REPAIRS NECESSARY AT THIS TIME

_____
_____

_____

ESTIMATE OF MARKET
VALUE_____

REPLACEMENT VALUE

_____

Summary of Surveyor's Opinion Of The General

Condition

_____
_____
_____

SAMPLE REPORT
Figure 6-2

SURVEY OF A RESIN 30, A 1980 FIBERGLASS CRUISING POWERBOAT BUILT BY A.B.C. MARINE, HULL NUMBER 123.

Date of Survey _____

HULL
1. The bottom of the keel is gouged from going aground and the aft edge is cracked on the centerline. Repair with epoxy glue and glass overlay, both inside and outside.
2. There are numerous deep pits in the propeller shaft and it should be replaced, along with the rubber shaft bearing.
3. The aft edge of the rudder is split on the centerline. Dry the glass rudder fill with epoxy and laminate three pair over the centerline.
4. There are some minor scratches in the topsides gel coat. There are some deep gouges at the stem.

DECK
1. There are some chips in the gel coat at the bow where the anchor is stowed. Fill with epoxy glue.
2. The vent cowl aft at the transom is at deck level and will allow water to enter. Suggest installation of a water trap type of ventilator.
3. The running lights were not working at the time of the survey. The masthead light is not in the forward part of the boat. The electronics were not checked with the exception of the VHF, which received normally.
4. There is no deck storage for the anchor lines, dock lines, fenders or life jackets (pfd).

5. The non-skid pattern in the aft deck is slippery.

6. The shore power plug is only on one side of the boat. If you dock port side to the dock, the cable will have to run across the deck.

MECHANICAL

1. The engine started easily and ran well but the forward, port engine mount is loose. Use a longer lag screw in the engine bed.

2. The exhaust line should be insulated from the engine to the collector.

3. Could not reach the shaft stuffing box. Install a floor hatch over.

4. There is no strainer in the sea water line to the engine.

5. The fuel tank fill pipe is not grounded to the bonding system.

6. Could not see the water level in the engine heat exchanger without using a mirror. Install a floor hatch over this fill cap.

INTERIOR

1. Install a shutoff valve in the gas line between the stove and the entrance door. This is in addition to the valves on the LPG bottles.

2. The vinyl hose on the toilet intake line is collapsed. Replace with a rigid hose and install a vented loop in the line.

3. The seacock for the toilet sink drain and the bilge pump discharge is frozen and cannot be moved. Replace seacock. Have a wood plug wired or chained to the valve. (Photo 9)

4. The area under the forward berths and forward of the forepeak bulkhead do not have any hull framing. Add stiffeners.

5. There are some water streaks on the hull in the wardrobe and there is no glass overlay at the deck to hull

joint. Tighten bolts at rub rail, caulk and install overlay on the inside, all around.

SUMMARY

The hull and deck are structurally sound except for the cracks at the rudder and at the bottom of the keel. This should be repaired immediately. Add stiffeners in the forward part of the hull.

The above are only samples. This information may be put in any form the surveyor finds easy to use while performing the survey or writing the report.

Photo 9   John P. Kaufman

This photo shows a tapered soft wood plug wired to the seacock with stainless steel wire. Bronze or copper window sash chain may be substituted for the wire.

INSPECTION OF THE LAMINATE

Fiberglass boats deserve a special kind of inspection as we try to determine if there are any internal flaws. The builder actually manufactures the material used for the hull shell and his skill and workmanship contribute to the integrity of the boat.

Other boat materials are purchased with the assumption of good quality and the builder concentrates on his own good fabrication techniques. When he buys aluminum or steel, the builder has to rely on the quality of the mill, as he very seldom inspects each plate. Of course, the wood builder checks each hull plank for knots and other natural flaws, and to be certain the plank has been cut with the correct alignment of the grain.

It is often very difficult to inspect the quality of the fiberglass laminate in a finished boat, as it is painted on the inside and the exterior has a color gel coat. Any accidents after manufacture would easily show as cracks or surface gouges, but the condition of the basic laminate is always in question.

There are three areas of particular concern when inspecting the hull: Thickness, Air Bubbles and possible Delamination.

THICKNESS

If the surveyor has a question about the thickness of the hull, he should consult with the designer, as the frame spacing must be considered at the same time. It is a mistake to generalize about hull thickness.

One guideline can be provided, however, and that is the minimum thickness required for resistance to impact loads. Every boat gets pushed against a piling at some time and a boat under thirty feet in length should have a laminate thickness of at least one-quarter inch at the sheer. The hull is thicker at the turn of the bilge, in the bottom and in the keel area. Longer boats have a proportionately heavier minimum thickness, as the weight of the boat is heavier and the impact loads are usually greater.

The hull thickness can be measured directly by removing some of the through hull fittings or hardware at the sheer or deck. Some surveyors have ultrasonic test equipment that can check the hull thickness when carefully calibrated. The surveyor is not usually asked to check the hull thickness, evaluate the content of the laminate or comment on the designer's specifications. His responsibility is solely to find the condition of the laminate and to report any deterioration.

A manufacturer checks the glass content of his laminates periodically by burning a sample that has been removed from the hull when a through hull fitting is installed. The sample is first weighed on an accurate jeweler's scale and then weighed after burning away the resin. The glass does not burn and its weight reflects accurately, the percentage of glass in the sample. Thirty percent glass content is average for hand laid up laminates.

BUBBLES

The laminators roll the glass plies against each other to insure they are saturated with resin and to remove any entrapped air bubbles. This is done with a roller made of stainless steel disks. Naturally, any air in the laminate forms a weak spot and they are difficult to detect.

If the inside of the hull laminate is not painted, you can look for air bubbles by putting a 500 watt lamp on the outside, assuming it is a solid laminate without a core. A good laminate shows an even texture and consistency of pattern, without spots or areas of a different color. Any entrapped air will show as white spots that are definitely different from the surrounding areas. A few, small, isolated bubbles are not of any concern, but a large area of air should be repaired. Normally, a repair can be made by drilling a small hole and injecting epoxy glue into the void with a glue syringe. This inspection is normally only possible at the builder's yard.

Where the laminate is formed over a relatively sharp corner, such as at the sheer or at the transom, there are very likely to be voids between the gel coat and the laminate. This happens when the laminators were not careful to roll the first layer of mat against the gel coat. The deck is particularly apt to have voids at the cockpit coaming, hatch openings and at molded toerails. These voids are usually found by the cracks in the gel coat and can be easily repaired with epoxy glue.

DELAMINATION

Delamination is the separation of the plies of the laminate normally caused by a lapse of time during the lamination, rather than working continuously in the lamination of one part. It may also be caused by dirt, water or excessive stress, both during and right after the curing process.

Frequently, delamination occurs in the deck when the core is not bonded to the laminate on either side. This is repaired by injecting epoxy resin through a small hole drilled into the core. Indications of this type of delamination are excessive flexing and a cracking sound as one walks on the deck. Beams should be installed under a deck that flexes.

The lack of laminate bond in the hull is hard to detect except by pounding on the outside of the glass hull with a rubber mallet or the side of a fist.

A solid sound will be heard where there is no

delamination and the laminate is not flexing. A dull thud and possibly a rattle will be heard when there is obvious trouble. Sometimes, a large area of delamination will have the two separated laminates banging against each other. If there is a large area without internal framing, you can flex the laminate by pushing in with a hand. Delamination will always lead to future cracking and failure.

EXTERIOR INSPECTION

You will find it takes little time to inspect the outside of a glass fiber hull that does not have damage. Looking for gouges, blisters and cracks and checking the flexibility takes about an hour on a forty foot hull. A much longer period will be spent on surveying the interior and the installed systems. This does not indicate the hull should be glanced over quickly, as there are often flaws in an otherwise glossy and fair surface.

When you first approach the boat, look for a high gloss on the gel coat, as a dull finish is a sign of poor molding or poor maintenance. The sunlight will eventually fade the gel coat, just as it does paint, and a new coat of wax should be applied twice each year.

Sight the sheer for a smooth, continuous curve as any humps show that the deck does not properly fit the hull. Vertical lines in the hull topsides occur where the interior bulkheads were fit too tightly to the hull. Such deformities can be avoided by laminating a pad of three layers of mat, about four inches wide, before the bulkhead is set into place.

It is difficult for the surveyor to decide what condition is cause for rejection and what can be tolerated for a long period of time. This applies to hull flexing, hairline cracks, corrosion and blisters. For example, can a one-sixteenth inch pit in a propeller shaft be overlooked but not a one-eighth inch pit? What if there is just one pit or twenty? If the gel coat has a hairline crack, will it progress into the laminate? These are hard questions to answer and it is probably best to conclude that any corrosion, pit or crack will probably increase to the point of causing a failure. It is the surveyor's job to point out these defects and assume the boat will have hard service, rather than just sitting at the dock. To be on the side of safety, we must always assume the worst and hope for the best.

FLEXIBILITY

We have discussed that a laminate which is too flexible may develop cracks and subsequent failure. Sometimes, a hull with a glass inner liner will not have the liner glassed, glued or overlaid to the hull and thus, the hull has no internal framing or support. Hitting the hull with a fist or a rubber mallet will reveal excessive flexing.

Normally, the boat will be sitting on blocks with some side supports where a flat spot will develop if the framing is not sufficient. If these side supports have screw jacks, you can extend them tightly against the hull while watching for any deflection. Be certain not to move the boat!

If the laminate has been damaged as a result of an accident, there will be hairline cracks in the gel coat. These will be circular at the point of impact and sometimes in a straight line, parallel to the stiffener about which the hull has been flexing. These cracks are easily visible from the outside, but detailed inspection on the inside is required to see if structural damage has occurred. Extra laminate may be required on the inside.

BLISTERS

Antifouling paint is always necessary on the bottom of a fiberglass boat if it is kept in the water. The paint manufacturer's instructions must be followed carefully. It is especially important to use the correct primer for the paint and to have the surface sanded clean and dry.

Blisters may appear on the hull bottom in the gel coat below the waterline and may be small or in clusters over portions of the bottom. It is not clear how these blisters develop, but there are probably minute pinholes in the gel coat formed at the time of spraying the gel coat into the mold. Possibly, a chemical reaction during glass lamination causes a gas pocket at the inside surface of the gel coat.

In the repair process, blisters are ground smooth and the interior laminate dried with a heat lamp. Epoxy glue is applied to smooth the surface, it is sanded smooth and a primer applied before painting. Many boatyards have developed specialized grinding equipment especially for blisters.

CENTERLINE SEAMS

Both the hull mold and the rudder mold may be made in two pieces that have a bolted flange along the boat centerline. This is done so the laminators can reach into all parts of the hull mold without stepping in the mold or laying on a scaffold. The rudder mold must be in two halves, of course, in order to laminate the inside. When the molding is completed and the two halves separated, the part is in one piece, but there may be some surface roughness and gel coat protrusions at the seam.

These centerline irregularities are ground smooth

and then carefully inspected to be certain there are no pits extending into the laminate. If so, the pits are filled with epoxy glue before grinding smooth and spraying with gel coat. It is very important to ensure this seam is watertight, as any pinholes will allow water to enter and destroy the laminate.

Powerboats less than 35 feet normally have bronze rudders, as they are readily purchased as off-the-shelf items. Larger powerboats and most sailboats use glass rudders in order to save weight and the lack of large bronze rudders. Glass laminates have taken over many products.

INTERIOR INSPECTION

The interior inspection of any boat requires an inspection of the forepeak area, the inside of the deck to hull joint, keel cavity, through hull fittings and joinerwork. No survey can be rushed, you must keep in mind that each square inch of hull surface must be inspected and evaluated.

The FORWARD AREAS are checked for any signs of cracking of the inside paint or laminate caused by excessive flexing. The hull sides are normally almost flat in this area with little stiffness resulting from curvature of shape. Longitudinal stiffeners from the stem to the forepeak bulkhead are always required with a maximum of 30 inch spacing.

When a boat hits a rock or is in a collision, it is usually the stem that incurs the damage, just at the waterline. With this in mind, it makes sense to have a watertight compartment or void, at the stem. It is not difficult to form a pyramid shaped box between the stem and the forepeak bulkhead, starting about two feet above the waterline. This may be filled with urethane foam, but must be glassed over at the top to be watertight.

The joint where the DECK MEETS THE HULL has been mentioned before, but must always be checked when the surveyor is inside the boat. This joint can not be overemphasized, as it is the primary source of water leaks created by the great abuse it receives when the boat twists in a seaway or hits a dock. (See Figure 4-7)

Whatever the configuration of this joint, it must be put together with caulking compound and bolted. The inside of this joint is overlaid with glass, not to make it watertight, but to stiffen the joint and help keep the bolts from loosening. Often, the rub rail bolts pass through both flanges of the deck and hull so a strong, watertight seam is formed.

On a sailboat, the shrouds put a large stress on the deck and hull close to the joint of the deck and hull. It is extremely important to laminate extra glass over the chainplate knees to both hull and deck so the rigging load is widely distributed. Water streaks inside the hull are signs the whole area of deck and hull around the chainplates has been flexing and more glass overlay is required.

Inspection of the KEEL CAVITY may be difficult due to tanks located on centerline, but there should be some access to see if water has accumulated. When the water has been removed, leaks or cracks may be found. If there are bolts for ballast or an outside, wood, grounding shoe, the bolts can be tightened after checking for leaks. A wood grounding shoe is probably better attached with an adhesive or epoxy glue. Often, a more thorough inspection of the keel area can be made from the outside.

When inspecting a THROUGH HULL fitting, it is the installation of this fitting that is most suspect and which causes the most problems. In many cases, the glass hull laminate is only one-quarter of an inch thick and rough on the inside to the point it is difficult to get a good watertight seal. In addition, the laminate can be over-stressed when a careless boatyard worker steps on the inside of the fitting and the attached seacock. This is especially true when a flush through hull fitting is installed that has a beveled edge on the outside flange.

It is good practice to increase the laminate thickness by fifty percent over an area of twelve inches square at all through hull fittings. Always have tapered wood plug wired or chained to the fitting. In the event of a failure, this plug can quickly be inserted into the damaged fitting or hull to lessen or stop the water flow.

When a critical inspection is made of the interior JOINERWORK, it is to judge the structural integrity and not just the beauty of the finish. All of the bulkheads, berth bottoms and locker sides are overlaid to the hull and form stiffeners to prevent hull flexing. This overlay of glass is called "secondary bonding", as they are glass attachments to the hull after the hull has been molded. To achieve a good bond, the hull and plywood surfaces must be clean and sanded to a rough texture. Often, these areas of overlay come loose with time, showing a lack of surface preparation.

All of the wood parts should be glassed to the hull or screwed to each other. Staples and nails are a sign of poor workmanship. If the joinerwork is assembled away from the boat and set on the wood or glass cabin flooring, they should be bolted and not screwed, as screws loosen from vibration.

The quality of the wood or plastic interior depends on the budget and the owner's requirements. The finest interiors have natural wood paneling over plywood bulkheads, with a fine varnish finish. Some people prefer a pattern provided by washable vinyl material, while the least expensive finish is just paint on the bulkheads and hull sides.

The surveyor should check any holes in the wood

bulkheads where piping or electrical wiring pass through. There should be a plastic bushing in these holes to prevent abrasion of the wiring or piping. When the wood joinerwork extends below the cabin sole, it should be glass to the hull throughout to form a watertight seal around the wood, as the wood will rot if water soaked. Paint alone does not provide sufficient protection.

Photo 9

The photo shows excellent use of wood joinerwork.

If the boat has an icebox, it should be surrounded on all sides with at least four inches of insulation. This is difficult for the surveyor to check, but he can sometimes see the area between the hull and the box. Any icebox drain should have a valve so cold water is trapped in the box to help the ice last longer. Many experienced skippers prefer to pump the water from the icebox directly overboard with a small hand pump or just a sponge. If a drain line is used to the bilge, bits of food may lay in the bilge with an undesirable odor.

There is always divided opinion about the finish on a cabin sole, which can be very expensive in teak or very plain in glass fiber. Whatever the material, it should be non-skid.

MECHANICAL SYSTEMS INSPECTION

In order to describe the survey of engines and equipment, each owner's manual could be duplicated and hundreds of pages could be written. But the surveyor really does not need this detail. It is sufficient to note if the equipment is operating properly and whether it is necessary to call a repairman.

For example, each engine has a lubrication system, a gearbox, exhaust line, controls and a fuel system. The surveyor should run the engine for a few minutes to check each function and to observe the overall operation. If there is any question, it should be noted with the suggestion that the boat yard conduct further checks.

The EXHAUST system is too often taken for granted, but it can show some engine defects at an early stage. If there is little water coming out with the exhaust gasses, there is danger of overheating and the water pump operation must be checked. Serious problems can result if exhaust gasses leak into the living areas. All exhaust line joints should be carefully checked for tightness. The line must be supported every three feet to prevent vibration. Mufflers must be replaced at the first sign of corrosion.

Even though the exhaust port at the transom is above the waterline, wave action at the stern can force water into the exhaust line, especially in a following sea. For this reason, all sections of the exhaust line must slope down from the high point at the engine.

Many problems with ENGINE COOLING are caused by restrictions in the sea water intake line. Occasionally, debris or a plastic bag will become lodged over the intake through hull fitting and it will have to be removed from the outside. I have seen a serious overheating problem as a result of weeds becoming wedged together in a reducing elbow fitting just at the water intake strainer. The strainer appeared perfectly clear and the problem was not noticed until all of the sea water intake piping was removed. This had to be done at sea in a 130 degree engine room. DO NOT use reducing elbows in any installation. If different pipe sizes must be accommodated, use straight reducing fittings. Any bends should be accomplished with bent pipe or gently curving hose. A seacock in this sea water intake line is vital.

The ELECTRICAL demand varies with each boat and the surveyor is not responsible for the size of the wiring or the circuit breakers. He is obligated to check the condition of the wiring, especially where it passes through bulkheads and joinerwork, to insure there has not been chafing. Circuit breakers, rather than fuses, should be installed in a central panel and there should not be more than one circuit wire to each circuit breaker.

Frayed insulation, lack of support for the wiring and wiring below the floorboards should be noted. There are many types of plastic clips on the market to secure the electrical wiring in neat bundles. The use of staples around the wire should be avoided. Often overlooked is the recommended practice of installing a circuit breaker within six feet of the exterior AC shore power supply plug, so all wiring within the boat is protected.

The Direct Current power supply is determined by the voltage of the engine starting motor and is normally 12 Volts D.C. in the USA. Separate batteries for engine starting and other boat circuits are recommended, both charged by the alternator on the engine. If the D.C. power supply is used continuously for radio communications, lights, stereo tape systems, speedometer, fathometer and other electronic gadgets, two or three batteries wired in parallel are suggested.

Electrical shorts commonly develop where there are water leaks, or due to improper installation. All the surveyor can do is report normal or faulty operation of the equipment. Owners and surveyors should read the standards published by the American Boat and Yacht Council, to remain current with the latest information on boat equipment safety.

The bonding system in a boat consists of a copper wire (#4) or strap running the length of the boat for attachment of the grounding wire of each piece of electrical equipment, the engine and the batteries. This insures the same ground potential throughout the boat and provides a permanent ground for the installation of any new equipment.

Larger boats may have AC generators so household type appliances can be used. Wiring and circuit breaker standards are the same as regional building codes, with the addition of wiring support and plastic sleeves, to prevent chafing when passing through bulkheads.

FUEL SYSTEMS

Most problems in any fuel system occur because of loose fittings in the piping, loose tank mounts or lack of support for the piping. Engine vibration requires a flexible piping section at the engine and fuel filters are necessary to trap any water or dirt pumped into the tank. The fill pipe on deck must be grounded to the tank and to the bonding system. This eliminates any spark of static electricity when the fuel hose on the pump touches the fill pipe on the boat.

All piping connections on the tank must be made on the top. There should be no openings on the side or bottom of a fuel tank. This reduces the possibility of draining the tank accidentally. Any transfer of fuel between tanks must be done with a pump and not by gravity feed. All tanks require a vent pipe to the exterior above the main deck, and a diesel fuel tank requires a return line for fuel flow from the engine to the tank.

All fuel tanks should have a shut off valve at the tank, as well as, at the engine. This isolates the piping in case of repair or accident. It also provides a theft prevention device if the owner shuts off the fuel at the tank when away from the boat.

Fuel tanks can be glass fiber, aluminum or steel and they must be separate from the hull. Integral glass fiber tanks that use the hull side and bottom as tank sides are not recommended. Vibration and impact against a dock may loosen the glass bond, resulting in a leak. Various types of plastics are used for fuel tanks, but manufacturer's instructions should be carefully followed to insure the tank is suitable for gasoline or diesel fuel.

FRESH WATER SYSTEMS

Plastic, glass fiber, aluminum or stainless steel can be used for fresh water, but they must be separate tanks that are well supported and not integral with the hull. Threaded nylon or bronze fittings should be used, as fittings attached with glues normally do not last. Aluminum or steel tanks should be coated on the inside with a special paint for water tanks. Plastic piping is in common use, but it must be reinforced to withstand the operating pressures of a pressure water system. It also must be able to be used with hot water and salt water systems.

If a hot water tank is installed, the heat is normally taken from the engine cooling system or from an AC electric heating element. This tank is subject to the same rusting as the tank in your house and the surveyor should carefully check for leaks at the tank and in all piping and fittings. Copper or sometimes PVC water piping is used and they both must be supported with pipe hangars, to prevent vibration and damage. A pressure water system provides additional piping and fittings to check.

STEERING SYSTEMS

Every boat should have an alternate method of steering, in case the primary installed system fails. Often, this replacement steering consists of a tiller and extension arm made from steel pipe which fits through a deck plate and attaches to the top of the rudder post. Even a small sailboat that has a wood tiller should carry an oar or paddle in the event the rudder fails. The primary steering system connecting the helm with the rudder may use a direct pipe linkage, a hydraulic system, a "push-pull" type of cable inside a sleeve, or conventional wire rope run over bronze sheaves. Different types of systems fit better in certain arrangements of boats.

If an autopilot is installed, the surveyor should determine if the equipment actually turns the rudder. The rudder blade should be observed while the helm and then the autopilot are turned. A mark on the helm should be checked to make sure when the rudder blade is actually amidships. Often, this is overlooked on new boats.

Photo 4

This photo shows the foundation and rudder collar which takes the weight of the rudder. Also shown is the hydraulic steering cylinder and second tiller arm for the linkage to control the other rudder. These items are not yet attached.

The entire steering system should be observed while the helm is being turned, to see if there are signs of binding, leaks or unusual noises. This is particularly important in a system using wire rope over sheaves. Any evidence of bronze powder or shavings means the sheaves are not aligned properly. The quadrant or tiller arm must be keyed to the rudder post and rudder stops must be installed to prevent the rudder blade from hitting the hull and causing damage to the steering gear.

If a rudder blade is lost at sea, a twin engine boat might get along with only one rudder, but a single engine boat will have to use a long steering oar as used on rowed life boats. The length makes stowing difficult, but the oar can be in two or three sections with a bolted section of pipe between. If the rudder is intact but the steering system fails, ropes might be rigged from eye fittings on the rudder to each transom corner. This may be crude, but it will give marginal rudder control in emergencies.

SUMMARY OF THE SURVEYING PROCESS

We have discussed the major items that are inspected during a survey, but can't begin to anticipate all of the items a surveyor may encounter. It is important to repeat the general approach: Look at each square inch of everything, determine if this is the correct material and then determine if the item has been installed correctly. Fiberglass hulls make the hull inspection easier, but we must still look for signs of delamination and water entry at the deck to hull joint, and at any through hull openings. Obvious dents and gouges show where further inspection is required.

New electronics are continually appearing on the market and it is hard to keep up with their specific operation. About all we can do is check for good operation and state whether or not it is normal. If there is any question about the proper operation, it is best for the surveyor to leave it alone and mention the particular equipment was not checked.

It seems obvious a more experienced surveyor may be able to do the job more efficiently and this is often true if that experience is with that particular hull material. However, the person who does the best job is the one who patiently looks at a small area and then proceeds to the remainder.

Chapter Seven

UNUSUAL SURVEY PROBLEMS

THE SUNKEN BOAT

When a boat sinks and is then floated, it is obvious any plywood, fabric or plastic laminate would be water soaked and would require replacement. Much depends on how long the boat was submerged. The engines and mechanical equipment are easily damaged by water, but if they are dismantled and cleaned quickly, they may be saved for future use. The hull and deck of any material are not usually damaged in a short period of underwater exposure, with the exception of water migration into the exposed edges of an unsealed laminate.

Certainly, most of the joinerwork and finishes would have to be replaced. Plywood and plastic laminates on countertops should be dried and then inspected, to determine the amount of water seepage into the edges.

One of the most troublesome problems with a sunken boat is the electrical systems. The batteries will be shorted out and a total loss and probably the engine starting motor, and the alternator as well. Electrical insulation around wiring may become water soaked by capillary action and all of the wiring may have to be replaced. Certainly all of the electronics can be considered beyond repair.

Unless you are unusually adept at rebuilding boats, it is probably best to stay away from a sunken boat. At the worst, everything will have to be repaired or replaced except the hull, deck, hardware, propeller, shaft, struts and the rudder. An insurance company settlement may make all the difference.

BALLAST UNDER THE BUNK

The surveyor was having a normal day on a large motor yacht when he looked under the bunk in one of the staterooms and discovered about 800 pounds of lead ballast, located outboard against the hull. The prospective buyer asked why the ballast was there and suddenly the survey became more complicated. A surveyor does not normally become involved in problems of trimming the boat, but this large amount of lead piqued their curiosity.

This is an example of when the boat must be viewed as a whole entity, in addition to the small details. The opposite side of the boat seemed normal on the lower level, but the main deck contained some heavy weights on the opposite side. The galley was on the main deck, together with a walk-in refrigerator and freezer, air conditioning systems, a large hot water tank and ten carbon dioxide bottles for the fire extinguisher system.

It was then revealed by one of the crew that the boat rolled excessively even in a calm sea. Putting all of these facts together, it became obvious the boat's roll was a result of excessive high weight, which raised the center of gravity. Also, there was too much weight on one side. It would have been a better design to place a stateroom on the main deck and locate all the heavy bottles, freezer, hot water and air conditioning on the lower deck, immediately above the keel. This was a round bilge hull which had a natural tendency to roll, even with the installed bilge keels. Careful planning, especially in a large boat, is always necessary to insure a successful vessel that will withstand the rigors of the sea through many owners.

EXHAUST FROM A "V" DRIVE

The surveyor ran the small gasoline engine while checking the operation and looking for oil or water leaks. The engine ran very rough both at idle and at higher Rpm's. On close observation, he saw arcing from the spark plugs to the exhaust line which had only been loosely wrapped with an insulating tape. The engine was installed to a "V" drive and the exhaust came off the forward end of the engine and made a 180 degree turn before running aft very close to the spark plugs.

A heavier application of fireproof insulation would have prevented this arcing of the spark plugs, but the proper installation of the exhaust line is the correct solution. A new exhaust line was fitted, leading to one side of the engine. Apparently, the arcing had not been noticed during the previous two years of operation and it was only the sharp eyes of the surveyor that found the problem. He was looking at the right place at the right time.

OPENING PORT LIGHTS IN THE HULL

A large motor yacht was being surveyed and the report strongly recommended the opening port lights in the hull side be replaced with the non-opening variety. These port lights were located in the engine room and in all of the staterooms, about thirty inches above the waterline. The surveyor was correct in noting the problem, as there have been cases where a boat went aground, heeled over, and water poured in the open port lights. The boat sank and a very costly righting and repair operation became necessary.

Ventilation to the staterooms and to the engine room should be provided by ducts to the main deck, rather than openings in the side of the hull. When electric power is available, fans circulate the air in each compartment.

Some years ago, there were a few occurrences of water entering the engine room of a sport fishermen through the air openings in the side of the hull. It was found that when the boat trolled at slow speed, in the trough of a wave, if an unusual wave rolled the boat to a certain extent, water would pour into the air openings. Keep all openings above the main deck. It is not difficult to install a duct from the house side, under a seat or counter and down to the engine compartment. It is also easy to install a fan in this duct.

PAINT MAY HIDE A PROBLEM

A surveyor was checking the inside of a glass hull in the lazarette where the hull shape was relatively flat and he noticed the paint on the inside of the hull laminate was cracked and flaking off in some areas. The first reaction was poor paint, or the surface was greasy when the paint was applied. He scraped away a large area of loose paint and then saw the glass laminate was white, indicating entrapped air between the plies of the laminate. A normal laminate would appear to be gray-green in color, a shade that only a glass fiber laminate can have.

The air in the plies could have occurred if the laminate was not well rolled out to saturate the glass and remove any air; the laminate was dirty or greasy when the next layer was applied; there was a change in the resin formulation; the laminate was not completed in one day and one ply completely cured before the next ply was added. Whatever the cause, this is an extremely dangerous situation for a glass hull, as the entire integrity of the designed strength is lost.

The paint had cracked on the inside surface, as the inside laminate was flexing independently of the outside laminate and the two portions of the hull laminate were literally banging together. If this were allowed to continue, cracks in the laminate would develop and there would be complete hull failure. The owner was fortunate the surveyor found the problem.

It is possible for this condition to develop in any area of the hull, deck or deck house structure. This is why quality control measures at the builder's plant are absolutely necessary, and this is why the surveyor or owner should sound all areas with a rubber mallet or the side of a fist. A rattling noise indicates some delamination is present, which should be repaired immediately. There can be no tolerance for an unsound structure.

Repairing a delamination in a glass structure is costly and tedious, no matter which of the two options are chosen. Grinding the laminate until the delamination is exposed is usually done only when the defect is close to the inside surface. Normally, small holes are drilled about one inch apart and epoxy glue is injected with a syringe. You can see where the glue fills the air pockets and bonds the two laminates together. This is continued over all of the affected area.

Chapter Eight

THE BUSINESS OF SURVEYING

This chapter will show some of the problems a surveyor has in obtaining his business and staying in this career. This will help the boat owner to be more familiar with the type of person he is hiring.

Basically, the surveyor is providing a personal service and sharing his knowledge and experience with the boat owner. Usually, a new surveyor will obtain work with another who has an established surveying business in order to learn the profession, both from a business standpoint and to gain from the years of experience of an established surveyor. This is not always an easy working relationship, as most people are not willing to pay a helper just to learn what to do. As with any job, it is best to have a friend or relative recommend you.

The qualifications to become a surveyor are many, as he should be prepared to answer questions about boat materials, engines, equipment, types of construction and electrical systems. The surveyor cannot be an expert in all fields, however, a sound general knowledge is essential. He certainly must be experienced in going out in a boat and with boat handling around the dock. He should read every book on cruising, boat repair, design and construction he can afford to purchase or borrow. The library and magazines are always good sources.

Boat repair yards are essential to the surveyor. He must be on friendly terms with all of the yard managers, as these are the people most likely to recommend him for future work. In addition, there is no greater importance than looking at many types of boats to discover what is right and what is wrong. Casual conversation with the yard manager and his workers will tell the surveyor what a builder did wrong, how a repair is accomplished and what new materials are being used to reduce boat maintenance.

Since the surveyor is providing a service to another individual, he must have a pleasant personality and the ability to get along with others. Sometimes humility is the best way to approach a problem. It is always reasonable to say, "I don't know" and then look at all the reference books and call knowledgeable friends to find the answer. Everyone in the boating business is a potential customer and the surveyor should be on friendly terms with all of these people in a fifty mile radius.

Surveying is not just looking at a boat and writing a report. Anyone who has their own business knows at least forty percent of your time is spent trying to find new business, and in public relations. "Out of sight is out of mind" is an old expression that certainly holds true for people who want to be successful in their own business. You must maintain contact with those people who are going to recommend you for a survey. Visiting the boat repair yards and boat dealers is necessary whenever you are not actually working on a survey. A great amount of knowledge is obtained in this manner.

One good method of keeping in touch is to write a quarterly, one page newsletter, in the form of a personal note addressed to a specific individual. No one pays much attention to a form letter addressed to "Dear Friends". The letter can be the same for everyone, but typed individually. In the letter you can mention you simply wanted to keep them informed of the activity in the world of surveyors, relay unusual surveys, tell of how many boats of what type were surveyed in the last three months and mention any frequent problems the general public should know.

The following is a short list of people who call or recommend surveyors. A successful surveyor will know these people and contact them frequently.

Boat Yard Managers	Marina Dockmasters
Boat Dealers	Yacht Club Dockmasters
Boat Supply Retailers	Insurance Agents
Boat Designers	Yacht Brokers

Any form of advertisement may lead to a client. Many of the above listed offices will have a public bulletin board where the surveyor can pin a few business cards to be taken by interested boat owners. Advertising in the classified section of newspapers and magazines has become too expensive, unless it is a small, regional newspaper, published weekly or monthly. Very often, these local papers do an excellent job in reaching the boat owners in your town and at affordable rates. It is a good rule to spend a week's gross income on advertising each year. As with any business, the best form of advertising is personal referral. It pays to have friends in business.

It is always hard to decide what amount to charge for a survey and you can't be influenced by other surveyors who undercut the fee, or by owners who complain they had another surveyor do a survey last year for fifty dollars less. In the long run, it is best not to work with these people. You know what your costs are and you have to pay for your car, advertising, tools, printing and the time for writing the survey report. It is best to charge the same hourly rate as the local plumber, auto mechanic, electrician or boat yard. If the boat owner wants a firm price, multiply the hourly rate by eight for a normal day's survey or by four if it is an in-the-water survey of a boat under thirty feet. Be sure to remind the owner that you have to charge extra for a second day of inspection and extra for travel if you are more than ten miles from the boat's location.

It is always good to join and participate in, any surveyors association that is active in your area. It looks impressive if your report and your stationery note that you are a member of these organizations. These groups do perform a valuable service as they screen prospective members to be certain they are qualified. They also provide the surveyor with news of unusual surveys around the nation, technical information and hints on how to conduct your business in an efficient manner.

If a person does begin surveying with an established company, it may be just on a part time, as needed, basis. This should be welcomed as valuable experience and an opportunity to make friends and become better known to the local boating community. The person you work for will become a very trusted source of information, referrals and assistance, should you later have your own surveying business. Most surveyors cooperate with each other on technical or business problems.

The surveyor usually has a complete set of tools in the car but carries only a few on board the boat. The clipboard, forms, flashlight and knife are in constant use, but you never know what problems may surface. Certainly, the surveyor should not scratch or damage any part of a boat unless there is a very good suspicion of a hidden defect. If paint is scraped, be certain the owner knows where to repaint. If blisters are cut open, make sure they are noted for repair, at the earliest opportunity.

In less populated boating areas or in Northern states in the winter, boat surveyors often have other jobs or careers that allow them free time to accommodate a survey whenever called. Some work as boat builders, boat sales persons or yacht brokers just to keep close to the activity on the boating scene. If a person has their own business, often they will have another business to occupy when one is slow. There are endless possibilities for working in boating if one is persistent.

Chapter Nine

EMERGENCIES

WATER RISING IN THE BILGE

The value of an automatic bilge pump with a float switch and 'on' indicator lamp is shown in a continuing water leak. When the indicator lamp stays on for more than a minute, you should certainly find the cause. If the leak cannot be found, a bucket may always be relied on to remove water as well as the pumps. It is also practical to have a "T" fitting, valve and hose in the sea water intake line to the engine. The valve can be opened to take suction from the bilge when the hull sea cock is closed. There is a large amount of water used by the engine and a small leak may be pumped dry in a minute. This condition will have to be watched carefully as the sea cock will have to be opened and the valve closed in the "T" fitting.

A loose hose clamp may have allowed a hose to slip off a sea cock or there may be a defective hose material and inspection in all compartments is certainly necessary. If the leak is from a sea cock and through hull, the leak problem becomes more troublesome. Sometimes tightening of the inside nut on the through hull fitting will slow the leak. If the seacock (valve) breaks or the hose ruptures and the seacock will not close, a tapered wood plug of soft pine may be inserted to stop water flow. The hose must be removed to insert the plug.

When the water leak is from a through hull fitting or from a crack in the hull, a collision mat may slow the leak to the point where inside repairs may be made. The mat is a five foot square of heavy vinyl or canvas, with a large grommet in each corner. Four lines, at least twenty feet long, are tied to each corner and the mat is slipped over the bow (or stern) with two lines on each side of the deck. The mat is positioned over the hole (source of the leak) and the four lines pulled tight and secured to deck cleats. Water pressure will hold the mat against the hull and the leak can be slowed. The effectiveness of the mat will be increased by sewing a one inch soft foam rubber strip about eight inches wide to the inside edges of the mat to act as a gasket. In olden days of wooden ships and iron men, the "gasket" at the edges of the mat was "baggy wrinkle." This was hundreds of short pieces of hemp rope permanently sewn into the canvas mat. The common use of "baggywrinkle" was to have it tied around the wire rope stays so the sails would not be chafed.

The first order of business when a leak occurs is to stop it or at least try to slow the flow. The collision mat, wood plug and rags may accomplish this to the point where underwater epoxy putty may be tried to stop the leak altogether. If the water flow cannot be slowed, you would certainly be in a dangerous situation and communications with the US Coast Guard would be necessary. It is important to keep the engine running so that the water can be pumped out with the intake line "T" fitting and it is even more important to locate the batteries above the engine so that they will not be shorted.

In an extreme situation, a boat less than thirty feet can possibly be rowed to shore if oars and oarlocks are available. If not, anchoring in fairly shallow water may be possible, with subsequent firing of flares in order to attract assistance.

MAKING THE BOAT UNSINKABLE

Foam flotation material can be permanently placed in the boat to make the boat unsinkable. The volume of the foam eliminates some of the storage space and it is a compromise to determine what is more important, safety or canned goods. Some areas of the hull are normally inaccessible and these can be used for placement of flotation material. These areas are outboard of the engine stringers and below the cabin sole and forward of the berths in the bow. Outboard and above each berth, the hull side is normally visible, but a trim piece can be brought vertically up from the berth to enclose flotation between it and the hull.

The amount of required flotation material must be carefully calculated for each boat, but an average glass hull would require forty to fifty percent of the displacement volume. That is, if a boat weighed 6400 pounds (100 cubic feet), we might expect 45 cubic feet of foam flotation. The material can be plastic foam of various types or end grain balsa coated with resin.

A boat designer would determine the amount of flotation by calculating the weight of every item in the hull and dividing by the density of that material to find the installed volume. This total plus the flotation material volume must equal or exceed the displacement volume. See Figure 9-1 for a more exacting calculation of flotation. Any flooding of the bilge should not be allowed to spread throughout the hull and the cabin sole and all bulkheads must be solidly glassed to the hull to make a watertight connection.

This example in Figure 9-1, a glass fiber, semi-enclosed powerboat, is similar to the boat shown in Figure 1-2. Two hundred pounds of flotation, with a density of 4.4 pounds per cubic feet are used to achieve full flotation. The displacement is divided by the weight of salt water (64 pounds per cubic foot) to find the required total volume of both boat material and flotation. Fuel and water are not calculated, as they are almost neutral in buoyancy.

Installing full flotation in any boat is work, but it gives a large margin of safety and is very reassuring to those who are uncomfortable around water. This does not mean that you should completely ignore other precautions. A trip offshore still requires a dinghy or inflatable raft, provisioned with food, water and flares.

A few custom and manufactured boats have been built with full flotation, but the extra cost seemed to be more important with the boating public than the increased safety. Maybe these were inexperienced people.

FLOTATION REQUIRED FOR A 28 FOOT GLASS HULL			
ITEM	WEIGHT pounds	DENSITY lbs/ft^3	VOLUME ft^3
Hull and deck	2,750	100	27.5
Deck house	250	100	2.5
Anchor/Cleats	50	490	0.1
Engine/Batteries	980	490	2
Helm/Steering	98	490	0.2
Exhaust/thru-hulls	98	490	0.2
Plumbing Electrical	120	490	0.25
Two Tanks (Alum.)	165	165	1

Fwd. Berths & Sole	240	40	6
Forward Head	40	100	0.4
Two seats at helm	240	40	6
Paint & Trim	180	100	1.8
Crew and Gear	689	100	6.89
Total Volume of Boat Material			54.84
Flotation Material	200	4.4	45
DISPLACEMENT	6100 / 64 = 95.3		99.84

Figure 9-1

LOSS OF STEERING

Assuming an inboard rudder, the lazarette should be checked to insure all the connections are sound and nothing is broken in the steering quadrant (tiller), tie rod (two rudders) or hydraulic cylinder. If there is a cable on sheave system or push-pull cable, be certain everything is intact. In the case that the rudder has dropped, the rudder collar has failed to provide support and wire will have to be tightly wrapped around the rudder post and secured to the deck beams to hold the rudder up and away from the stuffing box. This shows the necessity for a small hole or stout eye bolt in the top of the rudder post to which the wire can be secured.

If the steering system has broken, but the rudder itself is intact, the emergency tiller must be attached to the top of the rudder post. In a situation where the rudder blade has broken off the rudder post on a twin engine boat, only one rudder may do the job with a slight variation in Rpm on one engine.

On a single engine boat, a steering oar rigged to the

transom should prove to be adequate, but will require physical effort.

Another misfortune may involve a broken tie rod between the rudders on a twin engine boat. This can sometimes be repaired temporarily by using wood "splints" and the always important baling wire.

The above scenarios reinforce the need for a variety of tools aboard any vessel, if you are to make the necessary repairs.

SOME ADDITIONAL EMERGENCY EQUIPMENT
(Figure 9-2)

Wood plugs for all through hulls	Collision Mat & Ropes
Rags for stuffing in cracks	Steering Oar
Underwater Epoxy Putty	Rowing Oars & Oarlocks
Cloth backed tape (duct tape)	Plastic Buckets (4)
Aluminum & Steel Wire	Tools for the engine
1x2 & 2x4 wood, 6 ft. long	Engine spare parts
Hand Drill and bits	Boat Hook
Boarding Ladder	Three plastic flashlights
Dock & Anchor Lines	Batteries in plastic bag
First Aid Kit	Spare Compass
Radar Reflector	E.P.I.R.B.

Figure 9-2 shows a partial list of equipment required as "spare parts". This is in addition to the normal tool bag and the USCG required emergency gear.

LOCATION, LOCATION, LOCATION

If you must radio for help in any sort of emergency, you can't be helped if people don't know where you are. When you are within two miles of shore, it is usually easy to see your position, but when offshore it is vital to keep track of your movements on a chart.

Basic navigation calls for a dead reckoning (estimated position) found from boat speed and time on a particular compass course. Compass bearings of charted objects and points of land improve the accuracy of your location. Your limit of land sighting is about five miles, due to the curvature of the earth, but tall smokestacks and lighthouses may be seen at a greater distance. When offshore, a radio direction finder or other electronic navigation equipment can be used to verify the dead reckoning location.

The purpose of this brief section is not to discuss the various techniques of navigation, but to stress the importance of knowing your position at all times. A medical emergency, person overboard, or flooding requires assistance without delay and you should radio for help without taking time to figure out where you are. When there is an engine failure, you may need assistance, but time is not usually a critical factor.

The type of radio on board depends entirely on how far you plan to be offshore and the limits of your batteries and budget. Electronics specialists will be able to advise you of the best equipment to fit your needs. When you do not have battery power for communications, the last resort are flares and an Emergency Position Indicating Radio Beacon (E.P.I.R.B.). Don't go offshore without them!

Many boat owners ask about the differences in radio communications. A very simplified explanation is that the higher the transmitted frequency, the shorter the effective distance. For example, a television signal from a very tall antenna tower may be received 35 miles away on a normal TV antenna. This is a Very High Frequency (VHF) signal and a VHF radio may expect similar results, as a maximum. Lower frequencies, such as on a standard radio broadcast receiver may be received at much greater distances, especially at night. Whatever your onboard communications equipment, you still have to inform people of an accurate position.

FALLING OVERBOARD

Probably nothing is more frightening than falling overboard, and the best practice is to simply not go. U.S. Coast Guard statistics show that the majority of people falling overboard are men who have consumed some adult beverages and who are releasing that beverage over the boat's rail. Fortunately, most of the occurrences are in protected waters and end in quick recovery. When offshore, each person should wear a safety harness when on deck. The tether on the harness is clipped onto a cleat, padeye, jack line or eye bolt, placed at strategic locations at the helm and on the deck.

A life ring with a floating light is necessary for offshore and it should be thrown out immediately when a person goes overboard. This floating ring should be kept in sight every second as the boat is turned back to find the person. When the overboard is not seen by the crew, the boat should reverse course and proceed in the opposite direction until the person is found.

A real problem exists when trying to pull the person in the water back onboard. A boarding ladder is necessary for swimming and if the person is able to climb the ladder, but boarding is sometimes impossible for someone who is exhausted. A swim platform on the transom, a few inches above the water is always convenient, as a person can usually roll up to it. Many times it is necessary for another of the crew (with a life jacket on) to go in the water and tie a line around the person who fell overboard. He is then pulled up to the boat's rail and rolled onto the deck. A boat hook is very convenient in these circumstances.

BOAT THEFT

If someone cuts the dock lines and tows your boat with another, there isn't much you can do to stop them. Setting two anchors at the dock will slow them somewhat, but a towed boat always attracts attention and this theft is not common. There are some precautions that can be taken, in order to minimize boat theft.

Expensive electronics are often the target and they can usually be bolted to their shelf. Anything you can do to make the theft difficult may just deter a prospective thief. Jewelry, cash, important papers and portable items such as binoculars and small electronics can be placed in a hidden safe that is bolted to a bulkhead inside a locker. There are literally hundreds of places to hide items on a boat.

There is usually a main battery switch close to the batteries that selectively directs an alternator's charge to a certain bank of batteries. If this is turned to the OFF position when docking, it may slow any thief to the point where he leaves the scene. Another switch in the starting circuit, in addition to the normal key switch really confuses anyone not familiar with the boat. This switch can be hidden in a locker between the helm and the engine room. It's easy to be more clever than a thief.

When you leave the boat, turn off the fuel valves at the tanks and the valves in the fuel lines located in the engine room. When a thief cannot start the engine, they will usually leave, as they do not want to make excessive noise that will attract attention.

If the boat is kept on a trailer, all loose gear and valuables should be locked in a car or in the house. If you are going away for more than a few days and the boat is in the driveway, you might jack up one wheel of the trailer to put it on blocks and remove one wheel. An outboard motor can be chained and locked to the trailer around the lower unit and chained and locked to the hull at the motor mounts.

It is always money well spent to have a good insurance policy that covers the replacement cost of the boat when a theft occurs. Unfortunately, boats are seldom recovered after a theft, as they are quickly moved out of the state and often out of the country to be easily sold. If the trailer is at a storage yard or at a marina, it is important to know if there is 24 hour security that checks each boat and knows when a space or slip is supposed to be empty. People are often too busy to be on their boat every weekend, but the boat should be checked every few days for theft and bilge water.

In today's world of identically manufactured hulls, identification numbers on the transom and state registration number on the bow are sometimes the only distinction, in addition to the boat name. All of these are easily changed by a clever thief and it may be of some value for the owner to have some distinguishing features of their own. Federal government documentation of boats requires that the issued number be carved into a wood beam or forward bulkhead. An owner might do the same with a phrase or crest, just to make the boat easily identifiable if it is recovered after a theft.

On a glass hull, one owner sanded the laminate and put more laminate over a dollar bill, just to make his hull distinctive.

The easier the <u>mark</u> the more likely the theft will occur. The home security industry has a saying which I will loosely state. The higher the degree of security, the more dishonest the thief must be. No amount of security can provide 100% protection, it can only make the target less convenient to remove.

Chapter Ten

WHAT'S IN A NAME?

The person who is new in the boating world may sometimes be swamped with the names of various types of boats. This chapter will attempt to explain these vessels which are often combinations of other hull forms. In *Chapter One* we discussed hulls in the context of speed, length and the amount of accommodations on board. We will now go into more detail and look at the variations of styling shapes, above the waterline, that are called by different names.

Returning to the three classifications of the first chapter, any one may be displacement speed, medium speed or planing speed, dependent on horsepower. The cruising boats of today are designed and built for any speed.

The appearance of these boats, above the waterline, may also be anything that the owner requests, and the underwater shapes are designed to elicit the desired speed. The title of cruising boat applies to many different shapes.

THE OPEN BOAT

The basic open boat is usually less than 20 feet in length and can be called a canoe, garvey, kayak, rowboat, skiff, bateau, pirogue, punt, dinghy, pram or dory. They are usually rowed or paddled, but often sailed and they can be fitted with an outboard motor. The boat may be pointed on one or both ends and the bottom may be flat, round, or have a slight "V". Regional traditions often change the names and methods of construction. Throughout this discussion of boat types, there are always exceptions to any classification, such as the sailboard, gondola, or Polynesian proa. After the famous trip of the "Kon-Tiki", we might include the sailing raft in the list of unusual hull forms. We also cannot forget catamarans and trimarans, which may be designed to any boat type or hull speed.

Open boats are the most numerous in both sail and power, as the owner can enjoy the pleasures of boating at a minimum cost. The majority of sailboats are local fleets of a certain class, who have competitive racing around the buoys. A few of these classes are called Star, Laser, Lightning, Tornado and Intercollegiate dinghies. Small sailboats can be ballasted or unballasted and normally operate in a displacement speed mode. Some unballasted sailboats can achieve planing speeds if they are very light in weight and while sailing on a broad reach with a spinnaker. Catamarans and trimarans are good examples of high speed sailboats with light weight and a large sail plan.

Open power boats are usually of medium speed or planing speed and can include racing hulls, water ski boats, multihulls, fast fishing boats and fast passenger ferries. Open boats have no accommodations and are used mainly for short trips, just to enjoy the water. The open deck extends to almost full hull length and can be fitted to suit the owner's activities.

SEMI - ENCLOSED BOATS

This type of boat is very popular in lengths over 23 feet, as the cockpit is one third to one half the boat length and provides a large area for fishing or family fun. The forward half of the hull has a head and possibly berths for two. It can be designed for any speed range and is a balance between interior berths and exterior deck areas. The semi-enclosed boat is often built in lengths up to forty feet, as owners want the open deck for SCUBA diving, fishing or family swimming, yet still have some creature comforts for weekend cruising. This type of hull is definitely one for all purposes.

We seldom see sailboats with a very large open deck or cockpit, but there are some on the market for those who prefer day sailing with a group of friends. These hulls may be ballasted and fitted with an outboard motor.

CRUISING BOATS

Most boats over thirty-six feet in length fit this category, as these owners want the accommodations for living aboard and long distance cruising. The length of the hull merely reflects the owner's need for more staterooms and lounging areas. In the past, cruising boats were normally thought of as slow, displacement speed hulls. Recently, boats built for long distance cruising have been fitted with large diesel engines so that the hull approaches planing speeds. It has evolved that any sort of styling above the waterline may possibly be used with a bottom shape suitable for either displacement or planing speeds.

One cruising type of hull is the "trawler yacht" that is fashioned after a large commercial fishing boat. They are usually over 45 feet in length and of displacement speed (See Figure 10 - 1). Normally two feet wider in beam than a comparable length cruising hull, the trawler yacht has more inside space for living aboard. The open deck area forward can be used for a dinghy, SCUBA gear and deck boxes to stow the voluminous gear needed for cruising. A davit provides easier loading of the stores.

It is really styling that makes a trawler yacht what is. The distinguishing feature of the enclosed bridge above the galley and dining areas on the main deck show privacy and good visibility. The selection of this form of cruising hull is entirely the owner's choice of appearance and ease of handling of deck gear.

Figure 10-1

This illustration shows a 44 foot trawler yacht. Notice the unusual topside shape, open foredeck and enclosed bridge, often referred to as the "pilot house". This is a very popular live aboard cruiser style.

Returning to sailboats, most are cruising boats if they have accommodations, contrasting to open sailboats used just for an afternoon's sail. Larger boats have more berths with separate staterooms and heads. One type of cruising sailboat has evolved as the motorsailer, which has had many definitions and descriptions and which is an ideal form of cruising hull.

The motorsailer usually has a large engine, not only for propulsion at maximum speed, but for belt driven accessories, such as an AC generator, alternator, water maker or refrigeration compressor. It has a wider beam and higher freeboard, giving more interior room. The helm is usually enclosed in a deck shelter to keep out of the sea spray and the sail plan is relatively small for ease of handling. The owner has engine power to maintain a good speed when desired and a sail plan to provide the same speed in a fresh breeze. (See Figure 10-2).

This really is the most economical hull for long distance cruising. The large engine provides safety in an emergency and all the comforts of home, while the sails give constant propulsion with little regard for fuel supplies. Many people who live aboard like the motorsailer hull form for comfort and efficiency. Cruising doesn't get much better.

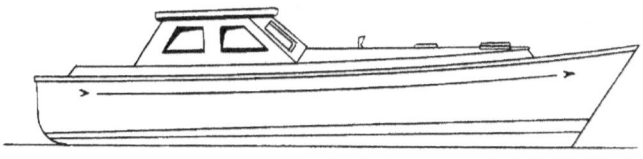

Figure 10-2

The motorsailer (shown here without the mast) can be distinguished from other cruising sailboats by its large deckhouse, wide beam, and higher freeboard. It has a large well-lighted interior for comfortable cruising.

The concept was carried to an extreme some years ago when a sailboat was marketed with a very large engine and the underwater hull shape of a planing powerboat. This provided very good speed under power as the hull no longer performed as other displacement speed sailboats. However, the performance under sail was somewhat restricted as the hull had greater resistance than one with a round bottom at slow sailing speeds.

Beating to windward is the slowest point of sailing and the motorsailer is primarily used under power when the desired course is directly to windward, assuming there is sufficient fuel. For long ocean crossings, the motorsailer concept is close to ideal.

Chapter Eleven

MAINTENANCE PROCEDURES

Fiberglass boats require some attention of a minor nature, but it is equipment inside the hull that usually demands the most maintenance. Whenever you are on the boat, it is a good idea to make a note of any items that need repair so you don't forget them when the boat goes to the yard. A separate list reminds you to buy any necessary parts both for repair and for spares.

It is primarily safety that demands good boat maintenance, and the following list shows some items that require attention. More detailed information may be found in the "Boat Repair Made Easy" series by John P. Kaufman (Bristol Fashion Publications, P.O. Box 20, Enola, PA 17025-0020).

MAINTENANCE LIST
Before Cruising & Monthly

HULL

1. Open and close all seacocks to insure proper operation. Check for water streaks on the hull which is evidence of a leak.
2. Check all hoses, especially in the head, to make sure all clamps are tight.
3. Lift all floor boards to check for water leaks.
4. Slide all drawers to make sure they are not stuck.
5. Check all around the sheer to look for water leaks.
6. Look for water leaks around sailboat chainplates. A hose can be used on the deck to determine any water leaks.

ENGINE ROOM

1. Check all oil drips or water leaks at the engine to determine the source.
2. Check the impeller on the engine and generator water pump.
3. Check operation of all bilge pumps.
4. Check oil level and water level in the engine and generator.
5. Check the water level in the batteries. Use a hygrometer to determine the state of charge. Insure there are plastic covers for all battery boxes.
6. Review all equipment instruction manuals and perform required maintenance.
7. Inspect all control cables and electrical wiring for corrosion and worn insulation. Make sure all support hangars are secure.
8. Inspect the steering system or cable for wear and corrosion. Check for leaks at the rudder post stuffing

box.

DECK

1. Check all cleats, chocks and stanchion bases for a firm mounting.
2. Check anchors and lines for ready deployment.
3. Check navigation lights, horn, flares, fire extinguishers and PFD.
4. Inspect the life raft and emergency food and water.
5. Make sure the boarding ladder is in place.

If you want greater safety and reliability, the maintenance will have to be faithfully accomplished on the boat and all of the systems. There is no substitute for checking every part of the boat every day while at sea. You can definitely prevent accidents from happening. The professional survey will give you a starting point in having everything in top condition. But it is your continued maintenance and inspections that keep the boat ready to sail at any time.

Chapter Twelve

ANSWERS TO YOUR QUESTIONS

Q My boat was in a collision and the glass hull is cracked in the bow area both above and below the waterline. Will you survey for damage repair?

A The first determination is how far aft did the water migrate and what damage was done to the glass laminate, joinerwork and electrical wiring. A repair procedure can then be written for the boat yard to follow.

The wiring is carefully inspected for any moisture on the insulation. Wet areas are cut off and new wiring is installed in its place. Lamp sockets will probably be rusted and should be replaced. If the wiring is inside conduit, the conduit will have to be removed for at least a six foot length to see if water has run between the wiring and the conduit.

Any wet plywood joinerwork will have to be replaced. The secondary bond of the bulkheads and berth flats to the hull can be checked with a putty knife to see if they are loose. Further overlay should be done with epoxy glue on a clean, sanded surface.

Cracks in the glass fiber hull will have to be cut out so there is a rectangular or round hole. The edges of the hole are tapered with a sander on the inside so the edge of the taper on the inside is about two to three inches from the hole. The laminate on the inside is sanded clean in an area about 24 inches from the hole. At this time it is extremely important to check the tapered laminate around the hole for any sign of moisture. It is possible for water to migrate by capillary action inside the laminate to some distance from the hole. If there is any moisture, the hole will have to be cut larger and tapered before any laminating can proceed. Two layers of glass cloth are laminated with epoxy resin over the hole, overlapping about two inches. Increasingly larger pieces of glass mat and woven roving are then alternately laminated until the repair laminate is twice the original hull thickness and the final layer of glass overlaps the hole about 24 inches.

After the laminate on the inside of the hull, the outside is filled with glass cloth, as necessary, and the surface made smooth with epoxy putty. Gel coat or paint can be used as the outside surface finish.

Q I've had three propellers on this boat and they don't seem right. How can I determine the correct propeller?

A The purpose of the propeller is to transmit the torque of the engine to thrust that moves the boat forward. To do this efficiently, the pressure on the propeller blade must be kept to reasonable limits and the total area of the blades is increased to keep the blade pressure to a minimum. Thus, a heavy boat requires a larger blade area than a smaller boat and the propeller diameter is increased in order to get this increased blade area.

When the same engine is used in both light and heavy hulls, with obvious speed differences, how do we efficiently use a larger or smaller propeller? The answer is, we change the propeller Rpm by using a reduction gear in the engine transmission housing. This reduction gear may be 1.5:1, 3:1 or 6:1 or any ratio in between. These ratios are the engine Rpm's divided by the propeller Rpm's. The slower propeller Rpm allows us to use a larger diameter propeller, with greater blade area, to keep the blade pressure low.

The propeller shop will provide you with the correct propeller size for your boat and engine. They often contact the propeller manufacturer in order to get propeller sizes for unusual situations. In all situations, the propeller diameter must allow maximum engine Rpm, but no higher. It may be well to mention that boat speed is solely determined by the boat's weight and the engine horsepower. The correct propeller size will produce maximum boat speed and the wrong propeller size will not. Changing the propeller size from the correct size will not increase boat speed. Take the manufacturer's recommendations and don't change them.

The pitch of the propeller blades is determined after the diameter is established and is primarily a function of boat speed and whether the hull is allowing the water to flow to the propeller in a smooth or turbulent manner. It is best to take the manufacturers recommendations, as changing the propeller pitch will not change the speed of the boat.

Q Can the surveyor tell me if my boat is seaworthy and will withstand large waves in the ocean?

A The word "seaworthy" is a general term often used to describe boats in advertising brochures. It must be defined in terms of wind strength and wave height in order to be significant. One could say a boat is seaworthy if it does not take on water after being subjected to a heavy pounding in rough seas. Unusual wind strengths and wave heights will damage many ships, no matter how many oceans they have previously crossed. After every typhoon, hurricane or whole gale, boats and ships are reported damaged or lost. Does this mean they were not seaworthy, or were the losses just unavoidable accidents?

If the hull laminate is adequate, the deck to hull joint is watertight and there are stiffeners to prevent the hull from flexing, the hull is usually a quality product. If the deck or cabin side flex when you push on the laminate, it is usually a sign that more stiffeners are required. Windows and hatches must be watertight and short trips in some rough seas will make any leaks obvious. Everything about the boat must be designed and installed to resist the effects of fatigue and the repeated application of high loads, such as pounding into a seaway.

If a boat is used primarily on protected waters,

rivers and small lakes and is not used in bad weather, it will probably have a long life without any structural problems. However, if a powerboat is run at high speed into five foot waves, one might expect the forward hull areas to be repeatedly stressed to the point of failure. These same areas may not be over stressed if the boat is operated at medium speed.

It is easy to see that the longevity of any hull is greatly determined not only by the quality of construction, but by temperate operation in rough seas. Many recreational boats sit at the dock for extended periods and are used less than 200 hours each year. Fiberglass boats will last a lifetime if they are not used! The same general thinking applies to sailboats, as the experienced skipper will know when to reef the mainsail and change to a smaller jib as wind strength and wave height increase. Safe operation includes protection of the hull and equipment on all boats.

Q Can I reduce the initial cost of buying a boat by obtaining a bare hull and deck and fitting out the interior myself?

A Yes, there are great labor costs that can be saved by doing all the work yourself, but you must have the time and be experienced both in handling boats and working with tools. Most people who build their own boats take great pride in their workmanship and in the accomplishment of a job well done. These are the motivating factors that ensure a successful project.

When discussing the costs involved, don't forget the rental of a building space and rental or purchase of tools. At some point, you will probably need the professional services of an electrician and an engine mechanic. With sailboats, one large expense is the ballast and the cost of transporting and lifting it to the hull. Moving the completed boat to the water and launching may involve thousands of dollars. Buy the hull delivered to your building.

If you purchase a bare hull, the molder should install some bracing across the beam to be certain the very flexible fiberglass hull does not bend out of shape. This bracing remains in the hull until the bulkheads are installed. The symmetry of the hull can be checked by fixing a string on centerline and measuring outboard to the sheers at the same longitudinal position. If a molded deck is installed on the hull before moving to your shop, the hull shape will be maintained, but it is more difficult to install the tanks, engine, generator and appliances.

After the bulkheads are installed, longitudinal stiffeners are overlaid to the glass hull and all joinerwork is secured to the hull in a similar manner. These all act as framing to reduce hull flexing and are very important.

If a molded deck is not purchased, it is possibly easiest to build a deck on top of longitudinal stringers that are set into notches in the tops of the bulkheads. The bulkhead tops are shaped to the deck curvature, less the deck thickness and are faired with the longitudinals so there is a smooth curve the full length of the deck or trunk cabin. Fiberglass or plywood and glass are then laid over the longitudinals to the required thickness.

The height of the deck is determined by the headroom requirements above the interior cabin sole. A string is stretched along the centerline at the deck height, marked on the bulkheads and a curve established from the centerline to the sheer.

The interior is drawn to scale on paper and large pieces of cardboard are cut to the dimensions of berths, counters, lockers, head, engine and everything in the hull. When these cardboard pieces are taped to the hull, you can walk around them and quickly see if any changes are necessary before cutting the plywood and finished trim. When the boat is completed, it is a good idea to hire a surveyor to check every part. You may have missed something and you also want to ascertain the integrity of the hull for your insurance company.

Q What type of bilge pump should I install?

A Every boat should have at least one manual bilge pump of ten gallons capacity, which can be permanently mounted and plumbed or have a long discharge hose to put over the rail. When the batteries or electric pump fail, it is wise to have a back-up. A bucket will remove water about as fast as a pump, but you may not have a place to dump the water if you are in the engine room.

Most owners like the convenience of electric bilge pumps, as they can be used with an automatic float switch to clear the bilge when the boat is unattended. The switch should be wired to a warning light or buzzer to indicate when the pump is in operation. If an unusually large amount of water is on board, the warning will show the pump is running continuously and the boat requires attention before the batteries are fully discharged. Bilge pumps should be able to move at least ten gallons per minute and they should be installed in each watertight compartment. Limber holes to allow bilge water flow were fine in wood boats, but safety calls for many watertight spaces in a glass boat to prevent flooding in a collision.

Q I go aground frequently and bend the propellers. Can I install a keel?

A Modern powerboats frequently have the propellers as the lowest point on the boat and sometimes "Y" shaped shaft struts will protect them. Better protection will result from installing a keel on the boat centerline. This is accomplished on a glass hull by sanding the hull clean for twelve inches on both sides of the centerline while the hull is supported by blocks on both sides of the bottom, away from the centerline. A foam core is cut to the final keel shape, extending from stem to within four feet of the transom.

It is not easy to laminate glass on a vertical or overhead surface, but this is essentially what has to be done to secure a new keel to a glass hull. The core is bonded to the hull with epoxy glue and is covered with glass laminate and epoxy resin to a thickness of one half inch at the hull bottom, and tapering to three quarters of an inch on the sides of the core. The bottom of the new keel should be two inches thick.

Before laminating, a two inch radius should be built with epoxy putty where the core meets the hull bottom. While laminating, check the straightness of the new laminations. Humps and hollows show poor quality. The glass applied to the hull bottom should be tapered so there is a smooth transition from hull to keel. When the glass has cured, the correct primer and the antifouling bottom paint are applied.

A deep keel is a very worthwhile and necessary part of the design of any boat, not only to protect the propellers, but also to help steer a straighter course in a heavy seaway. The bottom of the keel should be four to six inches below the bottom of the propellers. With a deep keel, the effectiveness and durability of an autopilot is greatly increased.

In areas of shallow cruising waters, many owners are aground frequently and they ask about protection for the glass hull or keel. In this case, we borrow an idea from the "worm shoe", used on wood hulls as a sacrificial strip of wood to keep worms from entering the main keel.

On glass keels, we can use a strip of greenheart, lignum vitae or even cypress, about two inches thick and as wide as the keel. It is glued to the glass keel with an underwater epoxy or a polyurethane adhesive. Be certain to support it well while the adhesive cures.

Q How can I repair bulkheads where the glass overlay is loose?

A The plywood bulkheads are usually attached to a glass hull with glass overlay, consisting of at least two mat alternating with two woven roving plies. This is called secondary bonding, after the hull laminate has cured. If the two surfaces are not clean or if the glass hull laminate has not been sanded thoroughly, this secondary bond of the plywood to the hull may be poor and will be subject to delamination as the hull is twisted and pounded by wave action.

When this lack of bond is detected, the old glass can be removed with a thin steel chisel, followed by sanding of the hull and both sides of the bulkhead, only where the glass overlay is loose. New overlay is then applied with epoxy resin, making sure it extends to a width of six inches on both the bulkhead and the hull. Make sure the top edge is secured to the underside of the deck. It is very important that the bottom edge of the plywood be watertight with resin and glass to prevent bilge water from entering the edge grain of the plywood.

If most of the bulkheads show loose glass overlay, it may be from poor workmanship, or it may be the hull does not have enough framing to keep the hull from flexing. The maximum unsupported span of the hull sides and bottom should be twenty inches. If this is not the case, the hull needs longitudinal framing made of solid glass about one inch wide and two inches high. These longitudinals are installed by first sanding the hull inside surface to a width of twelve inches where the framing will be located. Epoxy glue is used to locate a foam or glass laminate core and then glass overlay is formed over this core to the desired thickness and to a width of six inches on each side. Cleanliness and patience are the keys to a good laminate.

Bulkheads are not just partitions in the boat to achieve some privacy, they form a very important part of the structural integrity of the hull. The hull and deck form a box girder that resists the twisting, bending and pounding resulting from rough seas. But this girder must be reinforced internally by the structural use of bulkheads, longitudinal stiffeners and transverse framing. The attachment of these framing members to the hull and deck must be secure and permanent if they are going to do the intended job of preventing flexing. Glass material and various forms of resin attach themselves to each other with a chemical bond and both surfaces must be perfectly clean in order to get this bond.

Q Should I be concerned about going offshore with a large cockpit?

A If ocean waves are very large they can break over the rail of a boat and flood any cockpit area, whether on a powerboat or sailboat. Damage is done only when water enters the inside areas of the hull, through an open hatch or broken window. Common sense tells us to keep the hatches and doors closed when at sea and to have plastic or plywood covers for any large windows.

It is disturbing to have the cockpit fill with water and not drain out before the next wave dumps more on the boat. This usually happens only when traveling in the trough of large waves, when the cockpit drains are lower than the surrounding ocean. Altering course slightly to put the waves broad on the bow instead of on the beam may clear the cockpit when up on the crests of the waves.

If there are seat lockers in the cockpit, they are continually soaked with spray, and they must have tightly fitted gaskets and latches to prevent water from entering the hull. In addition, drain grooves at the edges will direct any water back to the cockpit. There should be four drains for the cockpit whether in a powerboat or sailboat and the sailboat must have seacocks where the drain passes through the hull.

When you are making long ocean passages, your concerns may be eased by tying a large vinyl cover from sheer to sheer over most of the cockpit length, so any water coming over the rail will be deflected aft and out over the transom. Maintaining a steady six to ten knots of speed in rough seas, on a course oblique to the waves, will go a long way to keep a minimum amount of water from entering the cockpit.

Q How can I reinforce a deck that is too flexible?

A A normal deck may have a laminate with three-sixteenths of an inch of glass laminate on both sides of a three-quarter inch, end grain balsa or foam core. If there are no transverse or longitudinal beams to support this laminate, it will be too flexible with the weight of one person.

The deck can be made less flexible by installing beams about twenty inches apart. If the headroom is limited, it may be better to install these beams longitudinally, starting at ten inches on both sides of centerline, but transverse beams may be used with the same twenty inch spacing. Any cosmetic headliner will have to be removed and the entire area sanded from one bulkhead to another, where the new beams will be installed.

A form or core, can be epoxy glued to the underside of the deck, over which the glass beam will be laminated. This core can be plastic foam or solid glass laminate. If the beams are transverse, the top of the core must be cut to the curvature of the deck. The glass overlay can be two alternating layers of glass mat and woven roving with a four inch width on the underside of the deck on both sides of the core. The final dimensions of the beam should be about one inch in width and two inches in height.

Additional beams are installed when it is not possible or convenient, to have a post supporting the deck, but a post provides a better structure. Many arrangements have a galley counter extending almost to the boat centerline or a sailboat may have a centerline table between sliding berths. These are good locations for a post from keel to deck.

Q What is the best shape for a hull?

A Powerboats that are slow in speed and sailboats, have a round bilge hull shape, as this gives the least resistance. Many sailboats have been built with a "V" bottom utilizing one or two chines and the results are not noticeable on a cruising boat. A chine is the intersection of the hull bottom with the hull sides, forming a sharp corner.

As the boat speed is increased, the boat goes through medium speed to approach planing speeds. Experience has shown the hull should be "V" bottom form for the greatest efficiency. A narrow beam produces less resistance than a wide beam, but the beam is primarily determined by the required width for the interior accommodations.

The angle that the hull bottom at the transom makes with the horizontal is called "deadrise angle", which is a strange term of undetermined origin. An average hull has a deadrise angle of about 12 degrees, but hulls designed for high speed in rough seas may have a 22 degree angle. "V" bottom hulls should have constant shape aft of amidships so the water flow is not twisted and exits cleanly from the transom. Multihulls may be of many different shapes, but all must provide a smooth water flow to the propeller.

Q Exactly what is the surveyor looking for on a sailboat?

A When working on a boat, the surveyor is the world's worst pessimist. He suspects everything has some defect or is not working and it is his job to determine the problem. No detail can be overlooked. As an example, when looking at the cockpit of a sailboat, he asks himself the following questions:

   a. Do the cockpit seat hatches have drain grooves to keep water from flowing into the bilge?
   b. Is the laminate of the cockpit sole and seats sufficiently rigid so there is little flexing when a person jumps on it?
   c. Is the cockpit sole braced to the hull with partial bulkheads?
   d. Is the wheel steering pedestal and guard rail through bolted with large backing plates? Is there a mark for rudder amidships?
   e. Are the cleats, fairleads and sheet winches through bolted with large backing plates, through solid laminate?
   f. Are the ventilator openings of the water trap type and are they properly ducted to the low point of the bilge?
   g. Are the stern rail bases through bolted? Are the individual sections properly welded or bolted?
   h. The backstay turnbuckle should be pinned to prevent rotation and there should be a toggle (clevis) just below the turnbuckle.
   i. Is the mainsheet traveler through bolted?
   j. Are there any voids, cracks or blisters in the gel coat?

On a sailboat, the surveyor is hauled up the mast to look for worn rigging, cracks in any welds and loose bolts. The spreaders are checked for signs of deterioration and loose attachment at the mast. Wire rope rigging terminals are inspected at both ends for cracks that frequently develop. On the deck, chainplates are inspected for wear and for secure attachment to the knees under the deck. At the bow of a sailboat or powerboat, the surveyor may spend twenty minutes looking at the following:

a. Are the cleats, chocks and anchor windlass through bolted with large backing plates?
b. Are there any gouges in the gel coat where the boat has hit the dock?
c. Are the lifeline stanchion bases and bow rail through bolted?
d. Do the sidelights in the bow rail light properly?
e. Are there signs of corrosion on the headstay turnbuckle?

Chapter Thirteen

FINAL THOUGHTS

Whether this is your first boat or the next of many, it is always wise to diligently check every aspect of the boat and her systems. You may have been extremely familiar with your last boat, knowing every sound and vibration it could produce. However, regardless of your boating experience, you will know little, if anything about the boat you are currently considering. Following the advice and procedures contained herein will surely provide you with piece of mind, knowing you have accomplished all you can to assure your next boat purchase will be an informed decision.

The surveyor may be tolerated but not appreciated by all but the buyer. The seller and broker do not want defects to become known which may cancel the sale. You will find hesitation from the broker when asking to board the boat to poke around in every area aboard. If reassuring the broker there will be no damage, does not receive a positive response, move on to another broker. Do not allow anyone to change your determination to thoroughly inspect the boat before making an offer. Your money and safety are at stake.

The survey and professional surveyor are a vital part of the marine industry. No insurance or finance company would consider a boat without a current survey.

The surveyor must know the limitations of many materials and what evidence shows deterioration. For example:

WOOD

Rots and splits. Plywood delaminates if the edges become exposed to water.

METALS

Steel rusts and aluminum oxidizes if not protected with the appropriate coatings. Bronze and copper also oxidize if not coated. All metals can develop cracks in areas of high stress. Close contact of dissimilar metals can cause corrosion.

PLASTIC COMPOSITES

If the edges are in water, delamination and failure will occur. The ultraviolet in sunlight will chalk many plastics if they do not have a protective coating with the proper inhibitors. Blisters may occur from faulty lamination practices.

Patience is the key to getting a good boat. Concentration on one small part of the boat allows the surveyor to determine if the correct material was used, properly installed, its condition, and if it must be repaired. It is a very methodical inspection of every portion of the boat that will benefit the buyer.

Good luck with your boat purchase and all your

boating endeavors. I hope you find, as millions have, that owning a boat is one of the most worthwhile, enjoyable investments anyone can make.

APPENDIX ONE

SUPPLIERS & MANUFACTURERS

The following list of Suppliers and Manufacturers in no way constitutes a complete directory of all the fine manufacturers and suppliers available throughout the country. This list does not recommend these companies, it should be used only as a reference. As always ask your friends for their recommendations. In most cases you will not be disappointed following their guidance.

SUPPLIERS

Boater's World: Boat Supplies 1-800-826-2628, 6711 Ritz Way, Beltsville, MD 20705

Boat/US: Boat Supplies 1-800-937-2628 880 S Pickett St. Alexandria, VA 22304

Defender: Boat Supplies 1-800-628-8225 P. O. Box 820

New Rochelle, NY 10802-0820
E & B Discount Marine: Boat Supplies 1-800-538-0775 P O Box 50050 Watsonville, CA 95077-5050
Home Depot: Tools/Supplies Located in most cities throughout the country. Look for them in your local phone books.
Jamestown Distributors: Boat Building/Repairing Supplies 1-800-423-0030 28 Narragansett Ave. P O Box 348 Jamestown, RI 02835
West Marine: Boat Supplies 1-800-538-0775 P O Box 50050 Watsonville, CA 95077-5050

MANUFACTURERS

Ameron Protective Coatings: Coatings, 800-926-3766, 201 North Berry Street, Brea, CA 92621
Apollo Diesel Generators: Gensets, 714-650-2519, 833 West 17th Street #3, Costa Mesa, CA 92627
Balmar: Alternators and Controls, 902 NW Ballard Way, Seattle, WA 98107
Caterpillar Inc.: Engines, 800-321-7332, P O Box 610, Mossville, IL 61552
Cummings Southeastern Power Inc.: Engines, 305-821-4200, 9900 NW 77th Court, Hialeah Gardens, FL 33016
Datamarine International Inc.: Electronics Instruments, 508-563-7151, 53 Portside Drive, Pocasset, MA 02559
Davis Instruments: Navigation instruments, 415-732-9229, 3465 Diablo Ave., Hayward, CA 94545
Detroit Diesel: Engines, 313-592-5000, 7215 South 228th Street, Kent, WA 98032
Espar Heater Systems: Cabin Heaters, 416-670-0960, 6435 Kestrel Road, Mississauga, Ontario, Canada L5T 128

Fireboy Halon Systems Division-Convenience Marine Products, Inc.: Fire suppression equipment, 616-454-8337, P O Box 152, Grand Rapids, MI 49501

Furuno USA Inc.: Electronics, 415-873-4421, P O Box 2343, South San Francisco, CA 94083

Galley Maid Marine Products, Inc.: Galley, Water supply and waste, 407-848-8696, 4348 Westroads Drive, West Palm Beach, FL 33407

Heart Interface Corp.: Inverters, Chargers, Monitors, Electrical 1-800-446-6180, 21440 68th Ave. South, Kent, WA 98032

Hubbell Wiring Device Division, Hubbell Inc.: Electrical products, 203-337-3348, P O Box 3999, Bridgeport, CT 06605

Icom America, Inc.: Electronics, 206-454-8155, 2380 - 116th Ave. NE, Bellevue, WA 98004

Indian River Battery: Rebuilt starters, alternators, motors, batteries, 561-562-3255, 3638 US Hwy. 1, Vero Beach, FL 32960

Interlux Paints: Varnish, Paint, Coatings, 908-964-2285, 2270 Morris Ave., Union, NJ 07083

Kilo Pak: Gensets, 800-824-8256, 190 S Bryan Road, Dania, FL 33004

Kop Coat Marine Coatings: Coatings, 800-221-4466, 36 Pine Street, Rockaway, NJ 07866

Marinco Electrical Products: Electrical products, 415-883-3347, One Digital Drive, Novato, CA 94949

Mercruiser: Engines, Drives, 800-624-2499, P. O. Box 1226, Waterloo, Iowa 50704

Micrologic: Electronics, 818-998-1216, 20801 Dearborn Street, Chatsworth, CA 91311

Nautical Paint Industries: Coatings, 800-432-4333, 1999 Elizabeth Street, North Brunswick, NJ 08902

New England Ropes, Inc.: All types of line, 508-999-2351, Popes Island, New Bedford, MA 02740

Northern Lights: Gensets, P O Box 70543, Seattle, WA

98107
Onan: Gensets, 612-574-5000, 1400 73rd Ave. NE, Minneapolis, MN 55432
Paneltronics: Electrical panels, 305-823-9777, 11960 NW 80th CT, Hialeah Gardens, FL 33016
Perkins Power Corp.: 305-592-9745, 5820 NW 84th Ave., Miami, FL 33166
Powerline: Alternators and controls, 1-800-443-9394, 4616 Fairlane Ave., Ft Worth, TX 76119
Racor Division-Parker Hannifin Corporation: Fuel filters, 800-344-3286, P O Box 3208, Modesto, CA 95353
Raritan Engineering Company, Inc.: Heads, Treatment systems, Charging systems, 609-825-4900
Ray Jefferson Company: Electronics, 215-487-2800, Main & Cotton Sts., Philadelphia, PA 19127
Raytheon Marine Company: Electronics, 603-881-5200, 46 River Road, Hudson, NH 03051
Resolution Mapping: Electronic charts and software 617-860-0430, 35 Hartwell Ave. Lexington, MA 02173
Sea Recovery Corporation: Water purification, 213-327-4000, P O Box 2560, Gardena, CA 90247
Seagull Water Purification Systems: Water purification, 203-384-9335, P O Box 271, Trumbull, CT 06611
Starbrite: Coatings /Sealants 1-305-587-6280, 4041 S W 47th Ave., Ft. Lauderdale, FL 33314
Statpower Technologies Corp: Chargers, Inverters, 7725 Lougheed Hwy, Burnby, BC Canada V5A 4V8
Teak Deck Systems: Teak deck caulking 813-377-4100, 6050 Palmer Blvd. Sarasota, FL 34232
The Guest Company, Inc.: Electrical components, Chargers, Inverters, 203-238-0550, P O Box 2059 Station A, Meriden, CT 06450
Trace Engineering: Chargers, Inverters, 206-435-8826,

5917 - 195th NE, Arlington, WA 98223

US Paint: Coatings, 314-621-0525, 831 South 21st Street, Saint Louis, MO   63103

Valspar: Coatings, 612-332-7371, 1101 3rd Street S., Minneapolis, MN   55415

Vanner Weldon Inc. Inverters & Chargers 614-771-2718, 4282 Reynolds Dr. Hilliard, Ohio   43026-1297

Webasto Heater, Inc.: Cabin Heaters, 313-545-8770, 1458 East Lincoln, Madison Hts, MI 48071

Westerbeke: Gensets, 508-588-7700, Avon Industrial Park, Avon, MA   02322

West System Epoxy: Gougeon Brothers, Inc., 517-684-7286, P. O. Box 908, Bay City, MI 48707

Woolsey/Z-Spar: Paint, Varnish, Coatings, 800-221-4466, 36 Pine St., Rockaway, NJ   07866

Yanmar: Engines, 800-962-1984, 951 Corporate Grove Drive, Buffalo Grove, IL   60089

Please mention this book when contacting the above companies.

GLOSSARY

This glossary has been compiled through a joint effort of the staff of Bristol Fashion Publications and many writers. It is not intended to cover the many thousands of words and terms contained in the language exclusive to boating. The longer you are around boats and boaters the more of this second language you will learn.

A

Accumulator tank-A tank used to add air pressure to the fresh water system thus reducing water pump run time.
Aft-Near the stern.
Amidships-Midway between the bow and stern.
Antifouling-Bottom paint used to prevent growth on the bottom of boats.
Arrangement Plan-The drawing that shows the berths, Galley and Head inside the hull.
Athwartships-Any line running at a right angle to the fore/aft centerline of the boat.

B

Backer plate-Metal plate used to increase the strength of a through bolt application, such as with the installation of a cleat.
Ballast-Weight added to improve sea handling abilities of the boat or to counter balance an unevenly loaded boat.
Beam-The width of the boat at its widest point.
Bilge pump-Underwater water pump used to remove

water from the bilge.

Bilge-The lowest point inside a boat.

Binnacle-A box or stand used to hold the compass.

Body Plan-The drawing showing the shape of the hull in an athwartships plane. Also called Sections.

Bolt-Any fastener with any head style and machine thread shank.

Boot stripe-Trim paint of a contrasting color located just above the bottom paint on the hull sides.

Breaker-Replaces a fuse to interrupt power on a given electrical circuit when that circuit becomes overloaded or shorted.

Bridge-The steering station of a boat.

Brightwork-Polished metal or varnished wood aboard a boat.

Bristol Fashion-The highest standard of condition any vessel can obtain and the highest state of crew seamanship. The publishing company which brought you this book.

Bulkhead-A wall running across (athwartships) the boat.

Butt connectors-A type of crimp connector used to join two wires end to end in a continuing run of the wire.

C

Canvas-A general term used to describe cloth material used for boat coverings of any type. A type of cloth material.

Carlin-A structural beam joining the inboard ends of deck beams that are cut short around a mast or hatch.

Cavitation-Reduced propeller efficiency due to vapor pockets in areas of low pressure on the blades. Turbulence caused by prop rotation which reduces the efficiency of the prop.

Center of Effort-(CE) The geometric center of the total sail plan on a sailboat. Used to determine lee or weather helm.

Center of Lateral Plane-The geometric center of the (CLP) underwater profile on sailboats used with CE, above.

Centerboard-A hinged board or plate at the bottom of a sailboat of shallow draft. It reduces leeway under sail.

Chafing gear-Any material used to prevent the abrasion of another material.

Chain locker-A forward area of the vessel used for chain storage.

Chain-Equally sized inter-looping oblong rings commonly used for anchor rode.

Chine-The intersection of the hull side with the hull bottom, usually in a moderate speed to fast hull. Sailboats and displacement speed powerboats usually have a round bilge and do not have a chine. Also, the turn of the hull below the waterline on each side of the boat. A sailboat hull, displacement hull and semi-displacement hull all have a round chine. Planing hulls all have a hard (sharp corner) chine.

Chock-A metal fitting used in mooring or rigging to control the turn of the lines.

Cleat-A device used to secure a line aboard a vessel or on a dock.

Clevis-A "Y" shaped piece of sailboat hardware about two to four inches long that connects a wire rope rigging terminal to one end of a turnbuckle.

Coaming-A barrier around the cockpit of a vessel to prevent water from washing into the cockpit.

Cockpit-Usually refers to the steering area of a sailboat or the fishing area of a sport fishing boat. The sole of this area is always lower than the deck.

Companionway-An entrance into a boat or a stairway from one level of a boat's interior to another.

Construction Plan-A drawing showing all the parts that make up the hull structure. The plan and profile are drawn.

Cribbing-Large blocks of wood used to support the boat's hull during it's time on land.

Cutless Bearing®-A rubber tube that is sized to a propeller shaft and which fits inside the propeller shaft strut.

D

Davit-Generally used to describe a lifting device for a dinghy.

Deadrise-The angle that a hull bottom makes with the horizontal. Measured in the aft part of the hull but more commonly at the stern. If the stern is flat from port to starboard, it has zero deadrise.

Deck Plan-A drawing showing all the structure and hardware on the deck.

Deck Camber-An arbitrary curve that the deck has from port to starboard.

Delaminate-A term used to describe two or more layers of any adhered material that have separated from each other due to moisture or air pockets in the laminate.

Device-A term used in conjunction with electrical systems. Generally used to describe lights, switches receptacles, etc.

Dinghy-Small boat used as a tender to the mother ship.

Displacement Hull - A hull that has a wave crest at bow and stern and which settles in the wave trough in the middle. A boat supported by its own ability to float while underway.

Displacement-The amount of water, in weight, displaced by the boat when floating.

Dock-Any land based structure used for mooring a boat.

Down Flooding-When water enters an open hatch or ladder.

Draft-The distance from the waterline to the keel bottom. The amount of space (water) a boat needs between its waterline and the bottom of the body of water. When a boat's draft is greater than the water depth, you are aground.

Dry rot-This is not a true term as the decay of wood actually occurs in moist conditions.

F

Fairing compound-The material used to achieve the fairing process.

Fairing-The process of smoothing a portion of the boat so it will present a very even and smooth surface after the finish is applied.

Fairlead-A portion of rigging used to turn a line, cable or chain to increase the radius of the turn and thereby reduce friction.

Fall-The portion of a block and tackle system that moves up or down.

Fastening-Generally used to describe a means by which the planking is attached to the structure of the boat. Also used to describe screws, rivets, bolts, nails etc. (fastener)

Fiberglass-Cloth like material made from glass fibers and used with resin and hardener to increase the resin strength.

Filter-Any device used to filter impurities from any liquid or air.

Fin keel-A recent type of keel design. Resembles an up-side-down T when viewed from fore or aft.

Flame arrestor-A safety device placed on top of a gasoline carburetor to stop the flame flash of a backfiring engine.

Flat head-A screw head style which can be made flush with or recessed into the wood surface.

Float switch-An electrical switch commonly used to automatically control the on-off of a bilge pump. When this device is used, the pump is considered to be an automatic bilge pump.

Flying bridge-A steering station high above the deck level of the boat.

Fore-and-aft-A line running parallel to the keel. The keel runs fore-and-aft.

Fore-The front of a boat.

Forecastle-The area below decks in the forward most section of the boat. (pronunciation is often fo'c's'le)

Foredeck-The front deck of a boat.

Forward-Any position in front of amidships.

Freeboard-The distance on the hull from the waterline to the deck level.

Full keel-A keel design with heavy lead ballast and deep draft. This keel runs from the stem, to the stern at the rudder.

G

Galley-The kitchen of a boat.

Gelcoat-A hard, shiny, coat over a fiberglass laminate which keeps water from the structural laminate.

Gimbals-A method of supporting anything which must remain level regardless of the boat's attitude.

Grommet-A ring pressed into a piece of cloth through which a line can be run.

Gross tonnage-The total interior space of a boat.
Ground tackle-Refers to the anchor, chain, line and connections as one unit.

H

Hanging locker-A closet with a rod for hanging clothes.
Hatch-A opening with a lid which openings in an upward direction.
Hauling-Removing the boat from the water. The act of pulling on a line or rode is also called hauling.
Hawsehole-A hull opening for mooring lines or anchor rodes.
Hawsepipes-A pipe through the hull, for mooring or anchor rodes.
Head-The toilet on a boat. Also refers to the entire area of the bathroom on a boat.
Helm-The steering station and steering gear.
Holding tank-Used to hold waste for disposal ashore.
Hose-Any flexible tube capable of carrying a liquid.
Hull lines-The drawing of the hull shape in plan, profile and sections (body plan).
Hull-The structure of a vessel not including any component other than the shell.

I

Inboard Profile-A drawing of the centerline profile of a boat showing the interior arrangement on one side.
Inboard-Positioned towards the center of the boat. An engine mounted inside the boat.

K

Keel-A downward protrusion running fore and aft on the

center line of any boat's bottom. It is the main structural member of a boat.

King plank-The plank on the center line of a wooden laid deck.

Knees-A structural member reinforcing and connecting two other structural members. Also, two or more vertical beams at the bow of a tugboat used to push barges.

L

Launch-To put a boat in the water.

Lazarette-A storage compartment in the stern of a boat.

Lead-The material used for ballast. Also, pronounced "leed", (as in leading a horse) when denoting the distance separating CE and CLP in a sail plan. (See above)

Limber holes-Holes in the bilge timbers of a boat to allow water to run to the lowest part of the bilge where it can be pumped out.

LOA-Length Over All. The over all length of a boat.

Locker-A storage area.

Log-A tube or cylinder through which a shaft or rudder stock runs from the inside of the boat to the outside of the boat. The log will have a packing gland (stuffing box) on the inside of the boat. Speed log is used to measure distance traveled. A book used to keep record of the events on board a boat.

LWL-Length On The Waterline. The length of a boat at the water line.

M

Manifold-A group of valves connected by piping to tanks. They allow filling and removal from one or more tanks.

Marine gear-The term used for a boat's transmission.

Mast-An upward pointing timber used as the sail's main support. Also used on power and sail boats to mount flags, antennas and lights.

Metacenter-A graphically determined point in stability calculations at one angle of heel.

Mile-A statute mile (land mile) is 5280 feet. A nautical mile (water mile) or knot is 6080.2 feet.

Mizzen mast-The aftermost mast on a sailboat.

Mold loft-A floor where hull lines are drawn full size. Patterns for construction are taken from the mold loft.

Moment of Inertia-Expressed as "I" in the units (inches^4). Indicates the resistance to motion (stiffness) of a particular structural shape.

Moment-A force (pounds) multiplied by the length of a lever arm (inches) to where the force is applied. (lb-in) If this is a rotating force on a shaft it is called torque or torsion. (lb-in). Bending Moment is the force applied to a plate or beam which tends to bend the beam or plate.

Moment of Inertia-Expressed as 'I' in the units (inches^4). Indicates the resistance to motion (stiffness) of a particular structural shape.

N

Nautical mile-A distance of 6080.2 feet

Navigation lights-Lights required to be in operation while underway at night. The lighting pattern varies with the type, size and use of the vessel.

Nut-A threaded six sided device used in conjunction with a bolt.

Nylon-A material used for lines when some give is

desirable. Hard nylon is used for some plumbing and rigging fittings.

O

Outboard Profile-A drawing of the outside of a hull. Sometimes called a styling drawing.
Oval head-A screw head design used when the head can only be partially recessed. The raised (oval) portion of the head will remain above the surface.
Overhangs-The length from the bow or stern ending of the waterline to the forward or aft end of the hull.

P

Painter-A line used to tow or secure a small boat or dinghy.
Pan head-A screw head design with a flat surface, used when the head will remain completely above the surface.
Panel-A term used to describe the main electrical distribution point, usually containing the breakers or fuses.
Pier-Same general usage as a dock.
Pile-A concrete or wooden post driven or otherwise embedded into the water's bottom.
Piling-A multiple structure of piles.
Pipe-A rigid, thick walled tube.
Planing hull-A hull design, which under sufficient speed, will rise above it's dead in the water position and seem to ride on the water.
Planking-The covering members of a wooden structure.
Plug-A term used to describe a pipe, tubing or hose fitting. Describes any device used to stop water from entering the boat through the hull. A cylindrical piece of wood placed in a screw hole

to "hide" the head of the screw.

Port-A land area for landing a boat. The left side of the boat when facing forward.

Prismatic Coefficient- (Cp) A dimensionless ratio of the hull displacement in cubic feet divided by the product of waterline length multiplied by area of the largest submerged hull section. (See text about Hull lines).

Propeller (Prop, Wheel, Screw)-Located at the end of the shaft. The prop must have at least two blades and propels the vessel through the water with a screwing motion.

R

Radar-A electronic instrument which can be used to "see" objects as "blips" on a display screen.

Rahola Criteria-Named after the person who proposed this measure of boat stability. Using a curve of Righting Arms at various angles of heel, the area under the curve to 40 degrees of heel must be 15 ft-degrees. (See text)

Rail-A non structural, safety member, on deck used as a banister to help prevent falling overboard.

Reduction gear-The gear inside the transmission housing that reduces the engine Rpm to a propeller shaft Rpm that is optimum for that particular hull and engine.

Ribs-Another term for frames. The planking is fastened to these structural members.

Rigging-Generally refers to any item placed on the boat after the delivery of the vessel from the manufacturer. Also refers to all the wire rope, line, blocks, falls and other hardware needed for sail control.

Righting Arm-A term used in stability calculations. The distance between the center of gravity of a hull and the center of buoyancy at one particular angle of heel.

Ring terminals-A crimp connector with a ring which can have a screw placed inside the ring for a secure connection.

Rode-Anchor line or chain.

Rope-Is a term which refers to cordage and this term is only used on land. When any piece of cordage is on board a boat it is referred to as line or one of it's more designating descriptions.

Round head-A screw or bolt head design with a round surface which remains completely above the material being fastened.

Rudder stock-Also known as rudder post. A piece of round, solid metal attached to the rudder at one end and the steering quadrant at the other.

Rudder-Located directly behind the prop and is used to control the steering of the boat.

S

Samson post-A large piece of material extending from the keel upward through the deck and is used to secure lines for mooring or anchoring.

Screw thread-A loosely spaced course thread used for wood and sheet metal screws.

Screw-A threaded fastener. A term for propeller.

Sea cock-A valve used to control the flow of water from the sea to the device it is supplying.

Section Modulus-Expressed as SM in the units (inches^3). Used in some formulas in place of "I", above. Indicates the resistance to motion (stiffness) of a structural shape.

Sections-Also, Body Plan. The shape of a hull in an athwartships plane, that is perpendicular to the waterline.

Shackle-A metal link with a pin to close the opening. Commonly used to secure the anchor to the rode.

Shaft-A solid metal cylinder which runs from the marine gear to the prop. The prop is mounted on the end of the shaft.

Shear pin-A small metal pin which is inserted through the shaft and the propeller on small boats. If the prop hits a hard object the shear pin will "shear" without causing severe damage to the shaft.

Sheaves-The rolling wheel in a pulley.

Sheet metal screw-Any fastener which has a fully threaded shank of wood screw threads.

Ship-Any seagoing vessel. To ship an item on a boat means to bring it aboard.

Shock cord-An elastic line used to dampen the shock stress of a load.

Slip-A docking space for a boat. A berth.

Sole-The cabin and cockpit floor.

Spade Rudder-A rudder that is not supported at its bottom.

Stability-The ability of a hull to return to level trim after being heeled by the forces of wind or water.

Stanchion-A metal post which holds the lifelines or railing along the deck's edge.

Starboard-The right side of the boat when facing forward.

Statute mile-A land mile which is 5280 feet.

Stem-The forward most structural member of the hull.

Step-The base of the mast where the mast is let into the keel or mounted on the keel in a plate assembly.

Stern-The back of the boat.

Strut-A metal supporting device for the shaft.

Stuffing box-The interior end of the log where packing is

inserted to prevent water intrusion from the shaft or rudder stock.

Surveyor-A person who inspects the boat for integrity and safety.

Switch-Any device, except breakers, which interrupt the flow of electrical current to a usage device.

T

Table of Offsets-The collection of measurements taken from the Hull lines at each section (or station). Used to draw the hull lines full size on the mold loft floor. It shows the waterlines, butts, sheer, chine in width and height.

Tachometer-A instrument used to count the revolutions of anything turning, usually the engine, marine gear or shaft.

Tack rag-A rag with a sticky surface used to remove dust before applying a finish to any surface.

Tank-Any container of size that holds a liquid.

Tapered plug-A wooden dowel tapered to a blunt point and is inserted into a seacock or hole in the hull in an emergency.

Tender-A term used to describe a small boat (dinghy) used to travel between shore and the mother ship.

Terminal lugs-Car style, battery cable ends.

Through hull (Thru hull)-Any fitting between the sea and the boat which goes "through" the hull material.

Tinned wire-Stranded copper wire with a tin additive to prevent corrosion.

Topsides-Refers to being on deck. The part of the boat above the waterline.

Torque (Or Torsion)-The rotating force on a shaft. (lb-in)

Transmission-Refers to a marine or reduction gear.

Transom-The flat part of the stern.

Trim-The attitude with which the vessel floats or moves

through the water.

Trip line-A small line made fast to the crown of the anchor. When weighing anchor this line is pulled to back the anchor out and thus release the anchor's hold in the bottom.

Tubing-A thin walled cylinder of metal or plastic, similar to pipe but having thinner walls.

Turn of the bilge-A term used to refer to the "corner" of the hull where the vertical hull sides meet the horizontal hull bottom.

Turnbuckles-In England they are called bottle screws. They secure the wire rope rigging to the hull and are used to adjust the tension in the wire rope.

V

Valves-Any device which controls the flow of a liquid.

Vessel-A boat or ship.

VHF radio-The electronic radio used for short range (10 to 20 mile maximum range) communications between shore and vessels and between vessels.

W

Wake-The movement of water as a result of a vessel's movement through the water.

Washer-A flat, round piece of metal with a hole in the center. A washer is used to increase the holding power of a bolt and nut by distributing the stress over a larger area.

Waste pump-Any device used to pump waste.

Water pump-Any device used to pump water.

Waterline-The line created at the intersection of the vessel's hull and the water's surface. A horizontal plane through a hull that defines the shape on the hull lines. The actual waterline or just waterline, is the height at which the boat floats. If weight is added to the boat, it floats at a deeper waterline.

Web Frame-The transverse structural members (frames) in a boat hull, installed port to starboard. Longitudinal frames are installed fore and aft.

Weight list-A compilation of every item in the boat. A calculation is made of the weight and center of gravity of everything on board. This is the only way a designer can estimate the displacement of the boat.

Wheel-Another term for prop or the steering wheel of the boat.

Whipping-Refers to any method used, except a knot, to prevent a line end from unraveling.

Winch-A device used to pull in or let out line or rode. It is used to decrease the physical exertion needed to do the same task by hand.

Windlass-A type of winch used strictly with anchor rode.

Woodscrew-A fastener with only two thirds of the shank threaded with a screw thread.

Y

Yacht-A term used to describe a pleasure boat of some size. Usually used to impress someone.

Yard-A place where boats are stored and repaired.

Z

Zebra Mussel-A small fresh water mussel which will clog anything in a short period of time.

Books published by Bristol Fashion Publications

www.wescottcovepublishing.com

Boat Repair Made Easy — Haul Out
Written By John P. Kaufman

Boat Repair Made Easy — Finishes
Written By John P. Kaufman

Boat Repair Made Easy — Systems
Written By John P. Kaufman

Boat Repair Made Easy — Engines
Written By John P. Kaufman

Standard Ship's Log
Designed By John P. Kaufman

Large Ship's Log
Designed By John P. Kaufman

Custom Ship's Log
Designed By John P. Kaufman

Designing Power & Sail
Written By Arthur Edmunds

Fiberglass Boat Survey
Written By Arthur Edmunds

Building A Fiberglass Boat
Written By Arthur Edmunds

Buying A Great Boat
Written By Arthur Edmunds

Outfitting & Organizing Your Boat For A Day, A Week or A Lifetime
Written By Michael L. Frankel

Boater's Book of Nautical Terms
Written By David S. Yetman

Modern Boatworks
Written By David S. Yetman

Practical Seamanship
Written By David S. Yetman

Captain Jack's Basic Navigation
Written By Jack I. Davis

Captain Jack's Celestial Navigation
Written By Jack I. Davis

Captain Jack's Complete Navigation
Written By Jack I. Davis

Southwinds Gourmet
Written By Susan Garrett Mason

The Cruising Sailor
Written By Tom Dove

Daddy & I Go Boating
Written By Ken Kreisler

My Grandpa Is A Tugboat Captain
Written By Ken Kreisler

Billy The Oysterman
Written By Ken Kreisler

Creating Comfort Afloat
Written By Janet Groene

Living Aboard
Written By Janet Groene

Simple Boat Projects
Written By Donald Boone

Racing The Ice To Cape Horn
Written By Frank Guernsey & Cy Zoerner

Boater's Checklist
Written By Clay Kelley

Florida Through The Islands What Boaters Need To Know
Written By Captain Clay Kelley & Marybeth

Marine Weather Forecasting
Written By J. Frank Brumbaugh

Basic Boat Maintenance
Written By J. Frank Brumbaugh

Complete Guide To Gasoline Marine Engines
Written By John Fleming

Complete Guide To Outboard Engines
Written By John Fleming

Complete Guide To Diesel Marine Engines
Written By John Fleming

Trouble Shooting Gasoline Marine Engines
Written By John Fleming

Trailer Boats
Written By Alex Zidock

Skipper's Handbook
Written By Robert S. Grossman

Wake Up & Water Ski
Written By Kimberly P. Robinson

White Squall - The Last Voyage Of Albatross
Written By Richard E. Langford

Cruising South
What to Expect Along The ICW
Written By Joan Healy

Electronics Aboard
Written By Stephen Fishman

A Whale At the Port Quarter
A Treasure Chest of Sea Stories
Written By Charles Gnaegy

Five Against The Sea
A True Story of Courage & Survival
Written By Ron Arias

Scuttlebutt
Seafaring History & Lore
Written By Captain John Guest USCG Ret.

Cruising The South Pacific
Written By Douglas Austin

After Forty Years
How To Avoid The Pitfalls of Boating
Written By David Wheeler

Catch of The Day
How To Catch, Clean & Cook It
Written By Carla Johnson

VHF Marine Radio Handbook
Written By Mike Whitehead

About the Author

Arthur Edmunds graduated from the U.S. Coast Guard Academy and completed his military service. After working at shipyards for a short time, he was a working designer for a leading boat manufacturer. He opened his design office in 1968 and has been busy ever since with a great variety of projects, not specializing in any type of boat or hull form. Repairs, rebuilding and engineering consultation have formed a large part of the design business. He believes in prowling boat repair yards where every problem in the world of boating is exposed for all to see and learn. Finding what goes wrong and what materials are best for a certain application is a very necessary part of a designer's portfolio.

He has crewed on ocean racing sailboats but also appreciates most people prefer to go maximum speed in powerboats. Successful designs have been completed for both manufacturers and individuals in all materials, and in all hull shapes. He has been residing in Florida since 1960 and now lives in Sarasota, FL.

Everyone hears strange and funny anecdotes about boats and men and Edmunds has a few tales to tell. He was standing near a tall, muscular winch grinder at an after race party who was mesmerizing a sweet young thing. The girl said she was amazed the spinnaker was set so high and wondered how it was done. The grinder happily replied, "We use spray starch."

www.ingramcontent.com/pod-product-compliance
Lightning Source LLC
Chambersburg PA
CBHW020356170426
43200CB00005B/197